IT'S ATTACHMENT

A New Way of
Understanding Yourself
And Your Relationships

MIROLAND IMPRINT 23

Guernica Editions Inc. acknowledges the support of the Canada Council
for the Arts and the Ontario Arts Council. The Ontario Arts Council
is an agency of the Government of Ontario.

We acknowledge the financial support of the Government of Canada.

IT'S ATTACHMENT

A New Way of
Understanding Yourself
And Your Relationships

Annette Kussin M.S.W., R.S.W.

MIROLAND (GUERNICA)
TORONTO • CHICAGO • BUFFALO • LANCASTER (U.K.)
2020

Connie McParland, series editor
Michael Mirolla, editor
David Moratto, cover and interior design
Guernica Editions Inc.
287 Templemead Drive, Hamilton ON L6M 2Z7
2250 Military Road, Tonawanda, N.Y. 14150-6000 U.S.A.
www.guernicaeditions.com

Distributors:
Independent Publishers Group (IPG)
600 North Pulaski Road, Chicago IL 60624
University of Toronto Press Distribution (UTP),
5201 Dufferin Street, Toronto (ON), Canada M3H 5T8
Gazelle Book Services, White Cross Mills
High Town, Lancaster LA1 4XS U.K.

First edition.
Printed in Canada.

Legal Deposit—First Quarter
Library of Congress Catalog Card Number: 2019946963
Library and Archives Canada Cataloguing in Publication
Title: It's attachment! : a new way of understanding yourself and your
relationships / Annette
Kussin, M.S.W., R.S.W.
Names: Kussin, Annette, author.
Series: MiroLand imprint ; 23.
Description: Series statement: MiroLand imprint ; 23
Identifiers: Canadiana (print) 20190161108 | Canadiana (ebook)
20190161116 | ISBN 9781771835183 (softcover)
| ISBN 9781771835190 (EPUB) | ISBN 9781771835206 (Kindle)
Subjects: LCSH: Attachment behavior. | LCSH: Interpersonal relations.
Classification: LCC BF575.A86 K87 2020 | DDC 155.9/2—dc23

*To my husband and my daughter
for their unwavering love and support.
Thank you for being my inspiration on my own journey
to becoming Securely Attached.*

CONTENTS

Prologue . . . . *ix*
Introduction . . . . *xiii*

Chapter 1: What Is Attachment? *1*
Chapter 2: Attachment in Childhood and Adolescence *13*
Chapter 3: Adult Attachment *31*
Chapter 4: Determining Your Own Attachment Classification . . . *51*
Chapter 5: Adult Attachment and Your Brain *65*
Chapter 6: Adult Attachment and Choosing a Partner *85*
Chapter 7: Changing Your Attachment Category *95*
Chapter 8: Other Important Attachment Concepts *131*
Chapter 9: Adult Attachment and Parenting *141*
Chapter 10: Conclusions *157*

Bibliography *163*
Acknowledgements *167*
About the Author *169*

PROLOGUE

I am a Social Worker/Psychotherapist. I became a Social Worker in
my early twenties. At that time, I wasn't interested in being a therapist. I wanted to be a Community Organizer and help people from the
inner city become a stronger force in the decisions that landlords and
politicians were making in their community. I did this for a number of
years. Doing such work was important and I felt that I was successful
in helping disadvantaged people find a voice in their community. It was
only in my later twenties when I began to work in a psychiatric hospital
that I realized that I had difficulty dealing with the strong emotions of
my clients. It was this realization that led me to enter therapy for the
first time. I joined a therapy group and realized after a few weeks that
I became somewhat of a co-therapist. Other members of the group
were able to share their pain and sadness, cry, get angry, and join in
all the exercises that promoted emotions. I thought all these exercises
were phony and useless and refused to participate. In one of these
games the other people in the group decided I would be the perfect
person to have on a desert island because I was so rational and calm;
not because I was an emotional support and sexually attractive.

I wish I would have realized then that maybe I was too rational, had
great difficulty being in touch with my feelings and expressing them,

had great fears of getting close to men, in particular. I was much more comfortable being on my own and focusing on my career, my hobbies, my fitness and my friends. It would take me many more years to recognize how significant these issues were for me. I did try a number of different therapies in my journey of self-awareness: group therapy, psychoanalysis, gestalt therapy and traditional psychotherapy. Most were helpful to some extent but none of them had a profound effect on my emotional expressiveness or difficulty with intimacy. I continued my patterns in relationships, which was to stay distant.

I developed my interest in Attachment Theory when I became the clinical director of a Children's Mental Health Centre. The theory helped me understand that the relationship between the mothers and children that led to these very young children being so challenging. I read about Attachment Theory, went to workshops on Attachment and then began working with Adopted Children and their Families from an Attachment Focused Model. I spent years developing my knowledge and skills in this model, working with Dan Hughes, a well-known specialist in Attachment, and other professionals. But the therapy was focused on the children and parents. I still didn't apply this to myself.

I became more interested in Adult Attachment and the different types of Adult Attachment in order to understand the parents of these adopted children and why they personalized the difficulties of their adopted kids.

As I read about the categories of Adult Attachment, particularly those developed by a researcher named Dr. Mary Main, I was startled to read about myself. All the behaviours that I demonstrated in relationships: my avoidance of the men I was interested in, my difficulty being in touch with feelings, my focus on my career, my valuing being smart and intellectual and my need to be active and busy were all described in one category of Attachment: Avoidant or Dismissing.

So now I knew what kind of Attachment I had and how I got to be this way. But how could I change this? There was very little in the books and articles I was reading that offered guidance on how to change one's Attachment Category.

There have been more books about this in the past 10 years but most of these are written for professionals. There are very few that are written to help people like you understand your Attachment Category and how to change it. This is why I have written this book.

Perhaps you also have difficulty becoming close and making commitments in intimate relationships. Or maybe you become dependent and demanding very quickly in relationships. Or perhaps close relationships terrify you.

All these problems are described in Attachment Theory. I hope you also will find yourself described in an Adult Attachment Category and suddenly have a new and profound way of understanding your personality and why you behave the way you do in relationships. I hope this book will bring that understanding to you in a useful way and offer you guidance on how to become a secure person with good self-worth, how to pick healthy partners/spouses and how to become a parent who passes this security on to your children.

I have offered ideas and guidelines on how to change the patterns that you know are problematic for you so you can develop mutually close, healthy and loving relationships.

INTRODUCTION

If you picked up this book, you're probably having problems in your relationship with your spouse, partner, boyfriend or girlfriend or perhaps a close family member. Or maybe you're feeling insecure and want to find a way of feeling good about yourself. You may have read other books on how to solve your relationship problems or your feelings of insecurity. You may have tried couple or individual therapy.

You may know some one who is struggling in a relationship and want to help. You may be just curious about yourself or others and want a new way of understanding your behaviour and that of others in relationships. Whatever reason motivated you to pick up this book, please keep reading.

This book is designed to offer you a new way of understanding yourself and the close relationships that you develop. I hope it'll help you understand why you chose the partner/spouse you did and why you react the way you do in your close relationships. I hope it'll help you be kinder to yourself, more understanding of your partner/spouse and change your harmful patterns in relationships.

This book is about a psychological theory called Attachment Theory. What is this? How is it different than other perspectives on relationships and on your sense of self? Attachment Theory believes that we come to be the way we are, have the personalities that we do and behave the way we do in relationships because of the way we were parented as infants and young children. There are other theories that have a similar belief and explanation about our way of being, but Attachment has some unique and valuable differences. The chapters in this book will explain more fully what happens in the early years of a child's life and how it continues to affect us as adults.

I want to share this perspective on understanding yourself and your relationships because it has been so valuable to me both as a professional therapist and as someone who has struggled in my adult relationships. I've been counselling and treating children, families, couples and individuals for over 40 years. I've been in my own therapy a number of times with different therapists using a variety of models of therapy, including Psychoanalysis, Traditional Psychotherapy, Gestalt Therapy and Group Therapy. Most were helpful and I did gain insight into myself and my challenges in relationships. None were based on Attachment Theory which would have been so much more helpful to me

I have also offered therapy to many many people throughout my career using different therapeutic perspectives and models. I have supervised and trained many other professionals. I was the Head of a Family Therapy Program and a Clinical Director of Children's Mental Health Agencies so also influenced the clinical direction of programs that provided help to children, adolescents and their families. Although I was familiar with Attachment Theory, I didn't understand it well or use the theory in my therapeutic work at the time.

As I look back on my career, I wished I would have known what I know now. If I could have translated my insights from Attachment Theory

to my clients, my students, my colleagues and organizations I believe
I would have created deeper and more lasting change.

I became more interested in this perspective on relationships when I
became the Clinical Director of a Children's Mental Health Centre for
preschool children. These children were very young but they seemed
so angry and unhappy, and already had significant problems in their
relationships with their parents, their peers, and their daycare staff.
What had happened at such a young age to cause these children to be
so troubled? The answer was very obvious. They had parents, particularly their mothers, who were also very troubled, and not able to meet
the needs of their infants and young children. These parents had significant challenges in their adult relationships as well.

Attachment Theory became more relevant to me in both understanding
and helping these young children and their parents. My interest in
learning more about the theory and its application in helping children
and parents led me to read the books and articles that were available
and to attend workshops by the leading people in the field. At that time
there wasn't a lot of information or training available.

Attachment Theory was developed by John Bowlby, a psychiatrist from
Britain. He and his colleagues, particularly Mary Ainsworth and Mary
Main, believed that infants instinctively communicate their needs to their
mothers or caregivers through their behaviour, such as crying, smiling,
waving arms and legs and making sounds. How a mother or caregiver
responded to these signals or behaviours determined whether an infant
would be securely or insecurely attached. Ainsworth and Main also developed research protocols to observe and document these behaviours. It
was Mary Main who also came to believe that the mothers already had
pre-existing patterns in their way of relating that affected their parenting. She developed the categories of Adult Attachment and how to assess
for these categories. I'll discuss these categories or types in this book.

I eventually became a member of a group of therapists who were studying with Dr. Daniel Hughes, a well-known Attachment Focused Therapist at the time. We would meet regularly, share our cases and consult with Dan. By this time, I was working with Adopted Children and their families, applying Attachment Theory in my understanding of the problems of these children.

The field of Attachment Focused Therapy changed dramatically during my years of applying it to adopted children. These children were extreme in their problems and traditional therapies were generally ineffective. There was much experimentation, innovation and research as therapists struggled to understand these children who'd come from orphanages or families where they experienced severe neglect and abuse. These children were often traumatized by their early experiences and had great difficulty trusting other adults who tried to care for them. They often presented controlling, aggressive, defiant behaviour or very dependent, needy, clinging behaviour. The dependent children were willing to attach to any adult who offered some attention. Working with such children was very challenging since they presented similar behaviour in their therapy with me. They wanted to avoid emotional vulnerability and found creative ways to do this.

When a child was adopted, I typically worked with the whole family, helping parents and the child to understand and express the feelings underlying the difficult behaviour. My goal was to help the parents create a safe environment for the child so he or she could risk developing trust in the new family.

Most parents had adopted believing they could offer a secure and happy family to the child or children. They couldn't understand why these children didn't appreciate what the new family was offering and change their distorted perceptions and mistrustful behaviour after receiving nurturing and loving care from their adoptive parents.

Some parents remained calm, patient and understood that their adopted children were mistrustful and hurting because of their experiences in orphanages and troubled families. They were able to use the interventions that I offered and understand that their adopted children needed years to gain trust. Others became angry, rejecting, blaming, and insecure about themselves. They couldn't use the understanding that their children were deeply affected by their early attachment or use the interventions I offered to help them parent. It became clear to me that their own history of being parented and their attachment as adults was being activated by their relationship with their adopted children.

I began to study more about Adult Attachment which at the time was an excellent theory but mainly used for research. I took a course to understand more about Assessing Adults for their Attachment type. It was a long and difficult course. I wasn't sure how it would help me with my adult clients. The course was very useful in helping assess and determine the Adult Attachment Categories from listening to, documenting and scoring the answers to particular questions about a person's childhood story. However, the course confirmed for me that information about Adult Attachment was mostly used as a research tool. The course didn't help me figure out how to apply this understanding to adults who were having difficulty parenting or having difficulties in themselves and their adult relationships. Yet, the descriptions of Adult Attachment made sense to me as a clinician. I could see Attachment behaviour in the parenting patterns of my clients, in the adults in individual therapy with me and in the couples I was treating in couple therapy. I knew I had to find a way to make it useful.

I began to explain Adult Attachment to my clients and reflect to them the type of Adult Attachment I believed they had. It not only made sense to me but also to most of my clients. It helped them understand why they were struggling with insecure feelings and with harmful patterns in relationships.

Most significant of all was recognizing my own Adult Attachment. It was clear to me that a number of the descriptive factors in the category of Avoidant or Dismissing Attachment applied to me. Both my challenges in relationships and my successes in life could be understood from the perspective of Adult Attachment. I felt deep regret that I hadn't understood myself and my clients from an Attachment perspective much earlier in my life and my career.

Over the years I have developed more understanding of Adult Attachment and created a model of therapy to use with individuals, couples and parents, based on Attachment. I teach this model to other professionals.

I've written this book in the hope that I can bring an awareness of Adult Attachment not only to people who are therapists and professionals in the helping field but to everyone who is an adult, a parent, a partner and a spouse. I hope that understanding the categories of Adult Attachment and how they affect your perception of yourself, your expectations in relationships, your patterns in relationships and the challenges of relationships and life will help you develop a new awareness. I'll also try and offer not only a new perspective but techniques and interventions, using this awareness, to try and make changes in yourself, your relationships and your parenting.

Chapter 1

WHAT IS ATTACHMENT?

∞

By the time we are adults most of us have experienced problems in our close relationships. You may be reading this book because you've been challenged by problems in your relationships and want to understand such problems from a new perspective. Such problems may have resulted in a difficult phase in your relationship that seemed to pass without a major crisis. Perhaps such problems created a crisis that led to being in therapy, or a trial separation or even separation and divorce. Or perhaps you've decided to remain in a poor relationship because you feel helpless and hopeless to change anything and leaving is too frightening and complicated.

You may be the kind of person who becomes anxious and angry in your relationship, feeling threatened by other people in your partner's life, feeling intense anger at your partner and feeling unable to control your emotions. Or maybe you're the kind of person who remains closed off from your feelings and has a difficult time telling your partner how you feel or what you need. Or maybe you feel scared much of the time, not trusting anyone and feeling chaotic inside.

You may not be in a close adult relationship because you have a pattern of finding the flaws in everyone you date. You're convinced that everyone you meet is just not the right person. But now you're getting older and the dates aren't flowing. You're lonely and longing to be in an intimate relationship and wondering how this happened.

You may try and blame your partners or your children for the problems in these relationships. However, there is usually some nagging voice from deep inside that tells you, you have a significant part to play in the problems. You may not acknowledge this to the people in your life, and even deny this to yourself but the self-awareness is lurking within you.

Most of us have tried to understand why we are the way we are, why we behave the way we do in relationships, why we repeat the same patterns with different people and why we parent the way we do. This looking at ourselves can be painful and sometimes brings on feelings that we're not good people. Although we may try and avoid such painful self-examination that honest inner voice holds us at least partly accountable for the problems we're experiencing.

Some of you have been in therapy, either individual or couple therapy or both. Your therapy may have involved a shorter term where you focused on changing your thinking and behaviour. It may have involved a longer period where you explored your history, your feelings and gained an awareness of yourself. You may have engaged in therapy with your partner/spouse and explored the harmful patterns in this relationship and how to change such patterns. Your therapy may have been helpful for a period but eventually the old harmful patterns returned. You may be feeling more discouraged and puzzled by this lack of change in yourself and/or your partner. Or the therapy wasn't helpful, either because you didn't feel understood by the therapist or the method of therapy didn't feel right for you and the problems you have.

A New Approach to Relationships

As I mentioned in the Prologue and Introduction, I want to introduce to you a way of understanding yourself and your relationships called Attachment Theory. It's not new in the professional field of child psychology and has been used for decades to understand and predict mother/child relationships and to understand children who have been adopted. But more recently Attachment Theory is becoming a way for professionals in the Mental Health field to understand adults, their perception of themselves, their relationships with their parents as adults, their patterns in their present adult relationships and their relationship with their children. It may be helpful to you in understanding yourself, understanding the feelings you have and how you express them, understanding your insecurities and self-doubts, understanding the patterns in your intimate relationships that leave you unhappy and unsatisfied and the ways you parent that you know are not good for your children.

So, What is Attachment?

Attachment is a deep lasting connection that develops between an infant and their primary caregiver, usually a mother, that develops in the early months and years of life. As you'll learn, it profoundly affects every component of human lives: mind, body, emotions, relationships, values and self perception. This deep connection operates at an unaware level in the child and later the adult.

It is a concept now used by researchers and therapists to understand the unconscious or unaware patterns that children and adults have in relationships. As I mentioned previously, it was developed by a British psychiatrist Dr. John Bowlby in the 1950s. He challenged the thinking at the time about personality development, Dr. Bowlby believed that all us were born to be in close relationships to survive both physically and emotionally. The theory continues to this day to help therapists and researchers understand what happened in the childhood of a person that resulted in his or her feeling secure or insecure as a child and as an adult. An adult's attachment category also influences his or her ability to parent children and develop secure or insecure attachment in the next generation.

Here's how Attachment develops. We are all born with the instinct to communicate our needs and wants to our caregiver. This instinct ensures our survival, both physically and emotionally. We need to be fed, have enough sleep, be cleaned and in a predictable manner in order to remain alive and be healthy. We need to be nurtured with love and care in order to thrive emotionally. So all babies are born with the ability to cry, smile, coo, laugh, and wave their arms and legs. These are the behaviours that tell a mother/ caregiver if they are unhappy and need to be fed, put to sleep, have a diaper changed or are not feeling well. Babies can also express to their mother if they are happy and content.

Most mothers/caregivers have the instinct to respond to the signals or ways of communicating of their infants. But some mothers/caregivers do not. So babies have to learn very early how to engage their mothers or caregivers so they'll feed them, take care of their basic needs and hopefully nurture them emotionally. Remember, if babies aren't fed and taken care of, they'll die. If they're not nurtured emotionally, they will die inside. The ways that infants learn to engage their caregivers stays with them at an unconscious level for most of their lives. What this means for you is that the ways you developed to ensure your parents or caregivers were close and took care of you are the patterns you continue to use to gain closeness to others. These patterns may be healthy or unhealthy but are your way of developing closeness.

I'm going to use the word mother or caregiver to refer to the person who is the primary person involved with an infant. In most societies this is the biological mother, since mothers give birth to children, are capable of breast feeding most of the time and are often home to care for their infants in the first few months. Also, infants instinctively reach out to their mothers for their biological needs and often birth mothers instinctively respond. However primary caregivers can be adoptive parents, foster parents, grandparents or hired caregivers in institutions and homes. Parents can be same sex couples where parents are male or female. Fathers now may also be the primary caregiver if their wives are the primary earner or the couple have an equal parenting relationship. Modern society brings other family structures, so mothers aren't necessarily the primary infant caregiver.

So, infants need to be close to their mothers or caregivers to ensure their physical and emotional needs will be met. The mother or caregiver who is connected to her infant, in time, figures out what the baby needs and wants by his or her behavioural signals. She or he will learn that a certain cry means the baby is hungry and that another cry will mean the baby is tired. A stressful cry will tell her/him something is making the baby very unhappy and she/he may spend more time trying to understand what is stressing the infant. This could be an upset stomach, an illness developing, a severe diaper rash or something that needs further exploring.

For those of you with children you may remember how you first responded to your baby's crying. You may have thought that the reason was the usual causes of an infant crying: wet diaper, hunger, being tired or not feeling well. At first you probably checked all these causes and eventually figured out what your baby needed. In time you probably learned the different types of cries and movements and what they signalled. I know that my daughter had a certain cry and would pull her ear when she was tired. I learned that if I let her cry for a short time, she would fall asleep.

But maybe your baby continued to cry even after you fed her or him, changed a diaper, and checked for anything that would be a discomfort. All you could do was comfort your upset baby. You may have tried various ways of doing this until you realized that a certain movement or way of holding your baby or certain soothing tones in your voice settled your baby. All of this would take some time but if you were a secure parent, you would do this patiently and calmly, until you figured out what your baby's cries were signalling and what you needed to do to meet your baby's needs.

My daughter, as an infant, went through a difficult few months where she cried non-stop. Nothing I seemed to do would calm or soothe her. My family doctor assured me nothing medically was wrong and that I needed to try various movements to soothe her. And so I did. I rocked her side to side, rocked her up and down and patted her back and stomach. Nothing worked until I tried rocking her up and down bending my knees. She stopped crying. My knees were killing me, but my baby was happy. I taught my husband and close friend the movement so when my knees were too painful they took over.

Knowing and feeling what's going on inside your baby and responding so the baby feels you get his or her needs and feelings is called **attunement**. The mother/caregiver who feels how stressed her baby is and uses her voice and emotions to communicate her awareness of her baby's emotional state and to soothe and comfort her baby is attuned. The attuned mother/caregiver also will express her joy and pleasure when her baby is happy and content. The mother/caregiver who figures out what her baby needs and is able to meet this need and comfort her baby helps her baby develop trust in the mother/caregiver. The more frequently this happens, baby signals its needs and feelings and mother responds accurately, the more secure and trusting the baby becomes. The baby feels understood and connected in a trusting way to her/his mother/caregiver. This is called **Secure Attachment**.

Even a good mother can sometimes not be available, so no one has to be a perfect mother. Babies give mothers many signals, usually by crying louder or waving their arms and legs if a mother misses the first communication of need. As long as the mother comes to her child in a timely manner and is able to comfort her stressed child, the infant will settle and trust its mother is available and attuned to its internal state.

However, when the main caregiver is regularly inconsistently available because of her or his own needs and moods, the infant becomes anxious, angry and confused. Sometimes the mother/caregiver is available and fully engaged with her infant so the infant does at times experience the closeness of the mother/caregiver. But frequently the mother/caregiver is not, preoccupied with her own issues and her unhappiness in her adult relationships. The infant tries to make its needs known by signalling more intensively, crying louder and louder, until the mother is forced to pay attention. That attention may be given with irritation, anxiety, anger and exhaustion. The baby doesn't experience the warmth and nurturing it needs to feel safe.

The mother's inconsistent availability leaves the infant feeling angry and anxious. The infant doesn't trust that its mother/caregiver will be attentive to its need to be fed, to have its dirty diaper changed, to be picked up from its crib, or attend to whatever the infant needs. Such infants long for the closeness and comfort of the caregiver but don't trust the caregiver will be regularly available. They demonstrate this by becoming extremely distressed when separated from their mother/caregiver but not finding comfort when they're reunited. Such infants feel very dependent on their mothers/caregivers, but this dependency leaves them feeling anxious and helpless and angry.

As the infants of such inconsistent mothers/caregivers become a little older they come to believe that they have to be very watchful of their caregiver's moods so they'll know when the caregiver is available. They also believe they must be intense and demanding in their communication to get the attention they need. Toddlers and school age children remain very dependent on these mothers/caregivers but also don't trust them to be consistent. They become angry when their mother/caregiver isn't available. They may yell, hit or bite their caregiver. Then they worry that they have pushed their mother/caregiver away with their anger. To pull the mother/caregiver closer again they become apologetic, cute and coy or even fake illness to ensure the caregiver takes care of them. This pattern becomes a very harmful one in the relationship. I call these children the push/pull kids. They pull their mothers/caregivers into being close and taking care of them by demanding and intense feelings and behaviour. They seem to be manipulative, but this is the only way they know how to ensure their needs for closeness will be met. But then their fear that they'll be rejected or neglected by the caregiver is activated and they push their parent/caregiver away. These children always feel angry and anxious inside.

Such children have **Anxious/Ambivalent Attachments**.

Let me give you a brief example. I had a client who was struggling in her marriage and feeling both very angry at her husband and very worried that he didn't want her anymore. I'll tell you more about her in other chapters. Although the marriage was precarious the couple decided to have a child. The wife came to see me on her own and brought her baby. She was so distraught and preoccupied by the struggles in her marriage and her mistrust of her husband she barely paid attention to her infant. When she arrived, the baby was sleeping but then woke up and began to fuss. My client initially ignored the baby, perhaps hoping she'd fall asleep again. The baby began to cry and my client looked annoyed at her child. She tried giving the baby a toy to distract her, but the baby only cried louder. She gave the baby a soother which quieted her for a while. Eventually the baby began crying very loudly, which meant the mother couldn't focus on her therapy. She had to attend to her baby, changing her diaper and finding a bottle for her. This was done with irritation, clearly signalling to this baby that her mother was not emotionally there for her and only attending to her because the baby demanded this. If this pattern continued and I suspected it would, this baby would come to believe that she had to demand that her mother pay attention to her needs and that she couldn't trust this mother to be available to her from her natural instinct to take care of her baby. This baby was developing an Anxious/Ambivalent Attachment.

When a mother/caregiver is rejecting, hostile, indifferent and unavailable, the infant/child learns to distance himself or herself recognizing he or she won't get needs or wants met in the relationship with the caregiver. Such infants come to avoid interaction with the rejecting or inaccessible caregiver. They push away any awareness of feelings, needs, wants since these will not be met by the caregiver. The rejection is too painful to feel.

Other children may figure out that by taking care of the parent/caregiver or being the perfect child they will be cared for or loved or at least receive attention and praise. Such care, love and attention still demands that the child deny or push away his or her own needs, wants and feelings and service those of the caregiver. Such children learn not to express vulnerable feelings, angry feelings or sad feelings. Children who have to be perfect hockey players or get straight A's to get their parents' approval are examples of this. They may appear to be strong and independent but this is based on a belief that they can't trust anyone to take care of them so they have to take care of themselves. They learn that they can't ask for help with their studies or can't tell a parent/caregiver that they are struggling with their hockey, football, swimming, music or whatever is challenging them. They will not receive the emotional support they need and long for. Such children develop **Avoidant Attachments**.

Let me give you another example from my practice. I worked with a family who came to me because of problems with their eldest daughter, as a result of being sexually abused. There were four children in the family, the youngest being a boy who was about three years old. In the second session, the mother was talking about herself, her problems with her parents and her problems with her daughter and husband. The three-year-old was trying to take off the top of a toy. He continued to do this on his own, although he clearly didn't have the strength or the knowledge how to do this. Neither parent noticed him struggling. At no time did he go up to either parent for help.

Eventually I asked if he needed help and he came to me. Even then neither parent brought him close to one of them to help. He let me take off the top and went off by himself, away from his parents and siblings to play with the toy. I felt sad for this boy and understood why the oldest daughter hadn't turned to her parents when she'd been abused. Both these children learned early on that their parents weren't available for comfort and support and learned to take care of themselves.

All parents/caregivers are sometimes not available because of outside demands on their time or even because of chores that need to be done. A parent may also not be available for one child because of the needs of another child who is sick or has special needs. A parent/caregiver may be in bad mood one day and not able to be emotionally available. Occasional unavailability by a parent/caregiver does not create children with Avoidant Attachments. Children develop Avoidant attachment when the parent/caregivers' unavailability or rejection of the child is consistent and part of the everyday life of the child.

Children who come from neglect or emotional, physical or sexual abuse are in a very confused state. A child instinctively would turn to a parent/caregiver for comfort and safety when they're scared or hurt. But if the source of the fear and pain is the parent/caregiver, what does a child do? Such children are conflicted by the desire to run to the parent/ caregiver for safety at the same time as the need to run from the parent/ caregiver. This is so confusing and disorganizing for a child. The child will either fight back, run or avoid the hurting parent or just freeze and do nothing. Some children will usually do one of the behaviours to protect themselves but some children are so scared and overwhelmed they do all of them at different times. These children have **Disorganized Attachments**.

I'll tell you about Marjorie later in this book. When she was three years old her father began to sexually abuse her. He started off by just touching and fondling her. Marjorie experienced this as loving and comforting behaviour. So, one day when her mother called for her she was about to reply and tell her mother she was with her father. Her father shoved her in a closet and told her sternly to keep quiet. Only then did Marjorie feel scared and know something bad had happened. She stood frozen in the closet, not saying a word to her mother. She was very confused. The touching that felt good and was done by her father, a man she was supposed to trust, had to be hidden from her mother. The touching continued and Marjorie learned to just freeze when it was happening and never tell anyone.

When this interactive pattern between the primary parent/caregiver and the child is repeated over and over again, it becomes the Attachment pattern that the child comes to know and expect. The child internalizes this pattern and it develops into a belief that the child has about what to expect in all relationships, how to perceive other people and how they see themselves. This belief is imbedded deep within the brain of the child and operates outside the awareness of the child. It becomes the template, not only for the parent/child relationship, but for all relationships. It's the default mode for the way the child will be in significant relationships. It's called the Internal Working Model in Attachment Theory.

This default mode operates unconsciously and continues to influence the way the child will be in relationships as an adolescent and later, as an adult. Attachment behaviour may look different as the child matures into an adult but continues to be based on whether the underlying belief about oneself is positive with trust in relationships or negative with mistrust about closeness in relationships.

You may be sceptical or even reject the idea that what happened in your relationships with your parents or caregivers is still influencing your relationships as an adult. This book will attempt to help you understand how your childhood experiences very much still live on in you. It will also help you understand how these influences more specifically apply to your present relationship patterns. And most important of all it will offer you both insight into your unhealthy patterns and practical interventions to change this.

What Attachment Theory tells us is that you can have a very harmful early childhood upbringing and still end up a secure adult. The good news is that, with the honest exploration of your childhood experiences, with the awareness of how your childhood affected you, with your grieving for what you longed for and never had, with your risking change in yourself and your present relationships, you can develop what's called "earned security." So unlike children who were given secure attachment by their loving secure parents, you'll have to earn yours by self-awareness and risking change.

The next chapters will help you better understand Attachment in Childhood and Adolescence and then in Adulthood. It will include some understanding of how Attachment is embedded in our brains and therefore influences us neurologically. I will tell you about clients I've worked with in therapy from an Attachment Focused Therapy model. The last chapters will focus on enabling you to change yourself and developing secure attachments in your adult life.

Chapter 2

ATTACHMENT IN CHILDHOOD AND ADOLESCENCE

ᕽ

Secure Attachments

We all want to feel secure, safe and loved in relationships. We all know that some children have this experience and others do not. Attachment Theory helps us understand what happens to children who feel this security and love and those that do not.

Infants and children who've had loving and nurturing caregivers, who were available most of the time, who figured out what their children needed and responded to their needs, who got pleasure from their children and were supportive when their children were upset, physically hurt or sick—develop Secure Attachments. These children will come to believe that they can trust most people, that close relationships are pleasurable and bring security and comfort, and that they're lovable and deserving of good relationships. They also know that, when they go out into the world, their parents are still available to them for comfort and support if they have problems or are frightened or sick.

Such children usually develop good peer relationships and positive relationships with teachers and other adults in their lives. They're able to develop good peer relationships because they value such relationships and are able to accept that other children may be different. They're usually non-judgemental, flexible and even able to accept some rejection without being devastated. If they experience challenging events in their lives that may be hurtful or undermining of their confidence, they're able to bounce back with support and encouragement from parents or other caring adults in their lives.

As secure infants become toddlers and develop language, they're able to express their feelings using appropriate words. As Secure children they're in touch with their feelings and able to express them without losing control. Such children are able to feel anger, sadness, anxiety and fear but not be over-reactive. They trust that if they express such feelings they will be heard and comforted by the adults in their lives.

Secure children are also able to comfort themselves when necessary. Young children can use stuffed animals, a special piece of cloth or clothing or other toys to comfort themselves before falling asleep or if they wake in the night and are not ill or frightened. Such secure children are able to use other adults in a healthy way for comfort when they are outside their home and something upsetting happens. They prefer the comfort of a parent but recognize that most other adults are safe and reassuring if a parent is not available.

Teenagers with Secure Attachments are usually socially, academically and emotionally successful. They begin to transfer their attachment relationships to other peers. Secure adolescents will usually choose peers to be friends or a romantic partner who are also healthy and successful. Older adolescents develop more mutual relationships with other peers where they each support each other and can negotiate and compromise. Secure adolescents are also able to bounce back after a romantic breakup. Secure adolescents may seek advice and comfort from other peers but will turn to their parents or caregivers if they are highly stressed and need adult support and comfort. They both respect authority figures and are able to challenge authority figures in respectful ways as they gain more independent thinking and a sense of morality.

Some time ago a former client referred her teenage daughter to me. This client had resolved her Attachment issues in her therapy. She was concerned because her daughter had broken up with her long-standing boyfriend and seemed depressed. I met with this girl, who was well dressed, a good student and who had many friends. She was very sad that her boyfriend had broken up with her. She was losing sleep and had lost some of her appetite, possible signs of depression. She acknowledged feeling rejected. However, she was talking to her friends who were very supportive of her. She continued to socialize and get pleasure in her activities. She was able to cry and feel sad but also regain control and talk.

In her therapy she was able to explore the relationship with this boy and recognize there were problems. After a couple of months, she felt resolved about this breakup, acknowledging both her part and her boyfriend's part in the problems that led to the breakup. I believed she would use this awareness to pick someone different in her next relationship. She was secure enough to bounce back from her feelings of loss and rejection.

This is what having a Secure Attachment in childhood and adolescence offers. This is what we would all want for our children and what we all deserved to have had in our own childhoods.

Anxious/Ambivalent Attachments

Children with Anxious/Ambivalent Attachments do not trust that adults and peers will be dependable and trustworthy. Because their primary caregiver was so unreliable, they're very sensitive to other people rejecting them and not being constant. They often misinterpret a friend's or adult's behaviour because of this sensitivity. They also have poor control of their emotions and react with intense anger if they even suspect that a friend or teacher or anyone in their life is not paying attention to them.

When they're in that state of anger, these children may say nasty remarks to a caregiver, teacher or friend, yell, or even become physically aggressive. The feelings of anger are so strong that any feelings of caring for or needing the other person are smothered. Once the anger has subsided and the feelings of needing and caring about the other person emerge, the child may be sorry for their behaviour and try and reconnect with the person they drove away with their anger. This may work initially with a friend or adult in their life but after many such angry episodes friends are driven away and teachers see this child as a problem in their class.

An example is a girl we will call Amy. Amy was eight years old and had a single mother who was inconsistently available. Her mother was constantly worried about what her boyfriend was doing and was on the phone talking to her friends and her own mother about her problems. Her mother had had many boyfriends and Amy could not understand why she couldn't just find one. She would get very angry at her mother but then would become scared that her mother would leave her. She just wanted to spend time with her mother and was so happy when her mother was in a good mood and they played games and watched TV together.

Amy had lots of problems starting when she went to daycare. She didn't want to leave her mother and would think about her often in the daycare, wondering what she was doing and why she couldn't be with her. She caused lots of problems at the daycare because she would get angry and misbehave. She tried to be good but when the daycare teacher paid more attention to the other children, she would do something to cause a problem so the teacher had to come to her.

Amy had many problems in school with other children and was not well liked. When a new girl, Patricia, came to the class, Amy really liked her. They became best friends and spent time together at recess and even after school. Amy was very happy until one day she came to school and saw Pat playing with another girl. Amy became very angry and without even thinking went up to Pat and said she hated her and never wanted to be friends. Pat was very surprised but told Amy she was really sorry, stopped talking to the other girl and spend the rest of the day with only Amy. However, when Pat told her mother what had happened, her mother said that it was important that Pat have other friends and thought Amy was being too "possessive." When Pat's mother could see that Amy was restricting her daughter, she began to invite other girls for playdates and eventually discouraged Pat from a friendship with Amy. Amy called Pat every day and tried to get her away from the other girls at school. She brought Pat candies and other gifts. Eventually she decided Pat was a jerk and stopped trying to be friends with her.

Amy continued this pattern with other friends and would also become angry at her teacher if she felt the teacher was not paying enough attention to her.

The dependent and demanding behaviour of children like Amy causes other children and adults in their lives to reject them, thus reinforcing their belief that they're not lovable and other people in the world can't be trusted to understand them and be there for them. By the time such children are adolescents this belief is so entrenched in their personalities it is very difficult to change.

By adolescence Anxious/Ambivalent children, like Amy, are having learning problems in school, are considered behaviour problems by teachers and parents and have significant conflicts with other teens. They have poor control of their emotions, present more aggressive behaviour, particularly when they feel neglected, are more manipulative in relationships and continue to be both dependent and mistrustful.

Amy, as an adolescent, would be desperate to be in a relationship but always vigilant about where her boyfriend would be and what he was doing. She would use her attractiveness and sexuality to ensure her boyfriend wanted her. She would probably become sexually involved with him as a young teen. If she thought her boyfriend was not available even when he was involved with school work, athletics or meeting with other people, she would become jealous, insecure and demanding. Her rage could become uncontrollable, resulting in her attacking her boyfriend or threatening to kill herself.

We could imagine this scenario with Amy as an adolescent.

Amy came to school and saw her boyfriend talking to another girl. She was instantly jealous, went up to her boyfriend and yelled at him that she never wanted to see him again. Amy could not concentrate on her work in the classroom and went home early. All she could think about was her boyfriend and the girl he was talking to. She felt a mixture of anger and devastation. How could he do this to her? When she figured her boyfriend was home she called him crying hysterically and told him she was going to kill herself. She felt that without him she had no reason to live. The first time this happened her boyfriend was reassuring and promised Amy that he wouldn't talk to this other girl. He convinced Amy that he loved her only and wanted to be with her. Amy calmed down and was happy again in the relationship. But this possessive and angry behaviour happened over and over again.

Eventually Amy's boyfriend, tired of her demands and emotional antics, terminated the relationship. Amy was left feeling abandoned, angry and even revengeful. She wasn't able to look at herself and take responsibility for her behaviour in the relationship. Initially she called her boyfriend constantly and even followed him. Finally she realized he wasn't getting back together with her and began flirting with other boys.

Allan is a young man I know who is constantly preoccupied with his live-in girlfriend. He has this ongoing fear that she'll cheat on him and become sexually involved with other men. His partner is a very attractive woman but has not cheated on him. She tries to assure Allan that she loves him, is loyal to him and committed to their relationship. Nothing she does reassures him for any length of time. He needs to know where she is, what she is doing and who she is with. When he can't contact her, he becomes extremely anxious. Friends have tried to reassure him as well, that his partner is committed to him and that he'll push her away with his jealousy. Although he knows this rationally, he is unable to contain his fears and anxiety.

We hear of such jealous and angry behaviour on the part of boyfriends, who have to know where their girlfriends are, what they are doing and demand that they have access to their girlfriends' iPhone and computers. We hear of such boys and men becoming aggressive toward their girlfriends, at times leading to serious harm or even death. These are extreme cases of Anxious/ Ambivalent Attachment.

Avoidant Attachments

Children with Avoidant Attachments typically do not come to the attention of school personnel. These children may be successful academically or the best in their sports or other activities and appear popular with their peers. They're not kids who ask for help or express strong emotions. They are usually the kids who will offer to help the teacher or other kids. They may become the leaders at the school and everyone believes they are well adjusted. It is very difficult to recognize that these are lonely and detached children with unmet needs.

Sometimes avoidant children are so quiet and withdrawn that teachers will notice them and show some concern.

More recently there has been more spotlight on such children or more on the parents. These are the parents who demand perfection in the performance of their children. The father who yells at his son to be better in hockey, who is furious if his child is not placed on the best team, who gets into arguments with coaches if they don't favour his son. Children of such parents learn that they have to be the best in their hockey teams, can't make errors, and can't show vulnerable feelings without arousing the wrath of their parent. They learn that they get approval, acceptance and attention by their performance not because they're unconditionally lovable.

Brian came to me as an adult at first because of marital problems. His wife complained that he was a nice attractive man but she never felt close to him. She tried many ways to get him to talk about feelings and his deeper thoughts but he seemed incapable of this. She left him once she was sure he would continue in therapy with me.

Brian had always been a nice quiet boy with a cheerful disposition. His parents never showed much open affection to him or said they loved him. Yet, he said that he knew he was loved. He wasn't a great student but always did his work and passed his tests so received the approval of his teachers and his parents. He didn't particularly excel at anything but was good in sports and most important was a good sport. Teachers always remarked what a nice cheerful boy he was and he was well liked by his peers.

He told me that he wished his father had spent more time with him when he was young. He would hang around his father when he worked in the garden or did repairs to the house. His father was a quiet man so they rarely talked but Brian was just happy to be with him. One time, he recalled, he was playing on a rock while his father worked nearby. Brian fell off the rock and hurt himself. He was in a lot of pain but said nothing. He hoped his father would notice. Although Brian really wanted to cry and go to his father, he just sat there holding in his tears and rubbing the side that was in such pain.

It was only later that evening when his mother noticed huge bruises on his arm and side that his mother learned that he had fallen off the rock. She put ice on it but even then Brian didn't tell her how much it hurt. And she didn't hug and comfort him and ask him why he hadn't come to her.

Brian came to believe that he had to take care of himself and that he had to be a cheerful boy who did not demand much of his parents or anyone else. He learned to bury any feelings of hurt, dependency, anger or longing for closeness. As long as these feelings were buried he got along fine with everyone.

In adolescence Brian was popular with his peers and certainly with the teenage girls. He was good looking, likeable, always seemed happy and easy going. He had no close friends. He usually had a girlfriend but these relationships didn't last too long. Whenever the girl wanted to be more emotionally close or wanted more of a commitment, Brian would end the relationship. He broke many hearts, he said, but always knew he could find another girlfriend. He did have moments, particularly after sexual encounters, when he felt this sad empty feeling inside but he always pushed it away.

I also remember another boy who must have been desperate but did not go for help. This case came to my attention when I was Director of a Children's Mental Health Agency treating adolescents. The agency was called to a school because a boy had committed suicide. We didn't know the boy before his death but pieced together some information about him and his life. Everyone was shocked by his death and it will become clear why no one realized how much pain he was suffering. The following is partly based on facts and partly what I believe happened to him to bring him to such despair.

Jeff was one of the most popular teens in his school. He was President of the School Council, captain of his football team and one of the best students in his school. His parents were very successful in their professions, proud of their son but rarely home because of the demands of their work. They often weren't in attendance at his games and missed teacher student meetings. They knew their son was a high achiever and not a problem at the school so didn't feel the need to attend such meetings. They always apologized to him but year after year they missed his games and school events. When Jeff was in his last year of high school he met a girl, Rachel, with whom he was smitten and for the first time became serious about a relationship. He had little time to be with her because of the demands from all his activities but tried to talk to her every day, even for a short time. To Jeff this was a significant commitment. They became sexually involved which Jeff did not do casually.

After months of being in the relationship Rachel said she wasn't happy. Jeff was shocked. He loved Rachel, thought they had a wonderful relationship and spent whatever free time he had with her. Rachel explained that she felt Jeff was not available, not just with his time but with his emotions. She said that whenever she tried to talk to Jeff about anything serious he would either avoid the discussion or make light of it. She felt he took nothing seriously, including them. Jeff was genuinely puzzled. He felt he was serious about Rachel and wasn't sure what she wanted from him. He assured her he would try harder but in fact Jeff was hurt and scared by what Rachel told him. Although he wanted to understand her complaints, he felt very anxious inside.

Instead of opening up to Rachel about his confusion and fears, Jeff became more involved in school politics and studied harder. He saw less of Rachel, not more.

Rachel ended the relationship a couple of months after the first discussion. Jeff was devastated but acted like he didn't care. He played football more aggressively but found it harder to concentrate on his studies. He dated many girls and had sex with most of them although he found little pleasure in his sexual activities. Jeff began to feel sadder and sadder but showed little of his pain and certainly didn't talk about this to anyone. He was sleeping less, not eating properly, partying and drinking more, and for the first time his marks dropped. Still no one at the school or at home seemed to notice Jeff's deterioration.

One early morning after Jeff left his latest sexual encounter, he felt such a deep sadness and emptiness he began to cry. He walked the streets that early morning feeling a deep despair. He still longed for Rachel, knew this was a hopeless cause and saw no future for him in any relationships. He came to the local bridge and stared down at the tracks below. He did think about what his killing himself would do to his parents and his sister but knew everyone would be fine without him. He wondered if and hoped that Rachel would miss him and be sorry that she broke up with him. With that thought Jeff jumped to his death.

Jeff is an extreme case of an adolescent with Avoidant Attachment leading to suicide. I want to ensure readers that most adolescents with Avoidant Attachment do not take their lives. But adolescence is a time when the brain is rapidly changing so feelings that may have been pushed away are not so easily repressed. Adolescence is also a time when teenagers have more stress and pressure from school expectations and from peers. Those teens that learned there's no point in going to an adult for support and nurturing may feel more isolated and vulnerable.

Also, teenagers, for the first time, develop more adult-like relationships with their peers. They develop more romantic relationships that include sexual and emotional intimacy. These relationships bring out all their insecurities and become more like the relationships they had with their parents as young children. They may feel they have to be perfect for the boyfriend or girlfriend, they may feel they have to take care of a boyfriend or girlfriend, they may feel they have to do whatever a boyfriend or girlfriend needs. Or they may simply keep their distances and not even develop a romantic relationship. Whatever type of Avoidant relationship they develop they would have learned that there's no point in expressing their needs, wants and feelings. No one would be available to listen and meet their needs. This is the sad belief they have.

His or her boyfriend or girlfriend may complain that something is missing in the relationship and that he or she needs more attention, more closeness and more sharing of emotions and information. Avoidant teens may feel more inadequacy in the relationship and genuine puzzlement about why their boyfriend or girlfriend wants more closeness. They certainly can't offer more intimacy since they're not capable of this. Feelings of sadness, loss and inadequacy may emerge and even be overwhelming. The Avoidant Attached teen may not be able to re-press such feelings in his usual manner. Teens who do reach out for help from either parents, other peers or school personnel because they're in such distress may experience understanding and comfort that can be life changing.

Because of Jeff's suicide the school invited the agency, where I worked, to put a worker in the school to be available to the students. In time many students who would not have turned to their teachers, peers or parents came to the worker to share their struggles. They could do this privately so the school staff did not know. This highly academic school that prided itself on sending most of their students to university had many Avoidant Children who needed emotional support. I hope we prevented other suicides by being available.

Disorganized Attachment

Children with Disorganized Attachments come from families or institutions where they experienced early losses, severe neglect, and/or physical, emotional or sexual abuse. They may have been abused by people outside their families but not protected by their parents. Children abused by the clergy, by coaches, by teachers and others also may develop Disorganized Attachments They see the world as an unsafe place and have deep mistrust of adults, particularly those in authoritative positions. They also do not believe that they're worthy of love and care and good treatment. Many such children have a deep sense of shame believing that somehow they caused their caregivers and people in authority to be so abusive to them.

Some of these children become victims in relationships tolerating other children to bully them, make fun of them and exploit them. Others become aggressors, ensuring they're safe from others by becoming invincible and impenetrable. They make certain that they're in control, do not trust others and challenge the authority of adults.

Such children frequently do poorly at school. They have trouble learning, get poor grades and behave badly. If children are worried about being abused by other people in their life or worried what will happen to them when they return home, they are not able to concentrate in school. This fear state does not allow the cerebral cortex, the rational part of their brains to develop fully. Without this part of the brain operating optimally the child or adolescent isn't able to plan, think abstractly, integrate information and make complex decisions all necessary for academic success. Fear and Disorganized Attachment create failing students.

Those children who become aggressive for self-protection are seen by the school as trouble makers and are often punished for their behaviour. Rarely do school personnel understand that underneath the aggression and anger is a scared child who anticipates that people will treat them badly. Punishing these children confirms for them that adults are untrustworthy and harmful.

By Adolescence such children have often been labeled serious school problems. They may become bullies or be the brunt of severe bullying and exploitation. Some teens with Disorganized Attachments join gangs where they know they'll be protected by the other gang members. Having a group of buddies who all see the world and authority figures as dangerous is very comforting to abused teenagers.

Marjorie was a woman I worked with as an adult. I mentioned her in my introduction. She told me her story in bits and pieces over the years.

Marjorie had been abused by her father sexually, physically and emotionally since she was a toddler. She didn't understand as a toddler why her father did what he did to her body and why he told her she could never tell her mother. She felt she must be doing something bad so kept the abuse a secret. She entered school a very confused frightened child who felt inside she was bad and dirty. She presented as a sweet compliant child always clean and well dressed. She had great difficulty concentrating at school always anticipating that when she went home she would be taken by her father to the bedroom where he would do bad things to her. Or she would fear her father yelling at the whole family with terrifying threats and at times physical punishment of her brothers. Marjorie loved her mother but knew she couldn't protect Marjorie or her siblings from the terror of her father.

The Catholic School System where Marjorie attended saw her as a sweet but cognitively limited child. They assumed early on that Marjorie would be placed in the non-academic stream where she would learn a trade.

As a young teen Marjorie was able to find the strength with outside support from a priest to confront her father and threaten him with telling the priest if he continued to sexually abuse her. The sexual abuse stopped but Marjorie continued to fear and hate her father. She emerged from the fog of abuse as a teen with no sense of self. She began to notice and pay close attention to the teens around her so she could learn how to act, what to wear and how to please everyone. She learned that, if she focused on the interests and lives of the other teens, they would like her and not learn anything about her. Despite having friends and doing better in school, Marjorie knew she was bad and dirty inside. She believed that if anyone found out about her abuse they would know that she was to blame and condemn her. She carried this secret deep within her. She was extremely vulnerable to being abused again.

Can Insecure Attachments Change in Childhood?

Children with Insecure Attachments can develop security if they're fortunate to find other caring adults who are involved in their lives with enough healthy frequency and intensity to make a difference. This adult can be a grandparent, other relative, teacher, coach, neighbour or therapist. Such adults become alternative attachment figures and can help children experience and internalize positive views of themselves and of relationships. They can compensate for negative child rearing experiences but only if they have frequent contact with a child. Many of us have heard someone we know say: "If it were not for my teacher, Mrs. Brown in grade 2, I would have failed school and had lots of problems. I knew she cared about me and tried to help me."

Since children spend so much time in school, teachers can play this role of alternative attachment figure. They can offer children the support, nurturing and structure that they need. They can be both loving and tough but with kindness and understanding. They are the people who can create opportunities for the "difficult" child to succeed, for the "too perfect child" to be spontaneous, and for the frightened child to feel safe and secure. Teachers can create a classroom that has all the qualities of a secure and safe attachment environment. It is not unusual for that abused child to disclose the abuse for the first time to his or her teacher.

I remember when I was seven years old my family moved to a new neighbourhood. I was terrified to start my new school. I was a shy frightened child but even by seven, I knew how to hide this and appear self-assured. The grade 2 teacher was very savvy and knew I was scared. She assigned a popular girl to introduce me to the other kids and stay with me during recess. This teacher made me feel safe and secure in her classroom and I knew I could go to her if I needed help. The transition to this new school was easy for me because of this teacher and the girl she assigned to assist me. This girl became my best friend for many years.

Unfortunately, more typically, teachers confirm for children their insecure attachment style since teachers get caught up in the difficult behaviour. The demanding whiney child who is loud and obnoxious will be reprimanded and sent out the classroom because he or she is so disruptive. The compliant achieving child will be rewarded and encouraged to be the perfect undemanding child. The aggressive and failing child who seems not to care may be perceived as a lost cause and whose absences are a relief to the teacher and the class.

It is challenging for a teacher with many children in her/his classroom to recognize that underlying all of these problematic behaviours are insecurely attached children. It is rare for a teacher to say to an anxious insecure child who is demanding and manipulative that she/he understands he's having a difficult time and that she/he will try and spend more time with him and then sit him near her for support. Many

teachers try and use their authority to reprimand and control a difficult child, when that child or adolescent needs more empathy and
support. Most teachers don't have an understanding of attachment to
use in their dealings with insecure and challenging children. Most
classrooms in the public system are large without extra supports, making it difficult for empathic teachers to offer individual support.

Grandparents who are closely involved with their grandchildren may
be alternative attachment figures. One client I had whose mother was
disturbed and emotionally abusive to her described going to her pater-
nal grandmother for lunch every day and often after work. This grandmother was affectionate and nurturing. She would offer comfort and
support by holding my client in her arms when she was upset and
talking to her. She knew she was loved unconditionally by her grandmother and internalized a positive view of herself although her mother was unpredictable and demeaning.

Another child, Jen, went frequently to her best friend's home where the
mother was kind and supportive. This mother knew that Jen's mother
was selfish and unavailable and provided a safe haven for Jen. Jen also
knew that her mother was not available and more involved with her
own difficulties and interests. She used her friend's mother when she
needed support or advice. She remained friends with this girl for many
years so the mother was available into her adolescence. Jen was fortunate to have maintained this friendship with the support of her friend's
family. Her friend's mother became an alternative attachment figure
for Jen, allowing Jen to internalize a positive view of herself and an
expectation that others could be loving and trustworthy.

Adolescents may find boyfriends and girlfriends who are so positive
and secure they shift the Attachment of the insecure adolescent. Let's
imagine that Jeff, the adolescent I mentioned in chapter 3, had a girlfriend, Rachel, who understood that he was frightened of closeness and

so was patient and gentle in encouraging him to open up and trust her. Let's suppose she was able to tolerate his need to distance her by his activities, not personalize this and use her friends and parents for fun and support when Jeff was unavailable. Perhaps in time Jeff would get more comfortable being close to Rachel, experience this closeness as comforting and pleasurable and be able to take more risks to share with Rachel his thoughts and feelings. If this relationship was long-lasting, in time Jeff might have come to believe that relationships did offer comfort and security and redevelop a secure attachment.

Adolescence is a time of significant neurological change and a great opportune time to help an insecurely attached adolescent to change. Although it seems that adolescents are more difficult, more challenging of parents and authority figures, and more interested in their peers and the peer culture, adolescents are more open to adults, other than their parents. This is a time when teachers, coaches, other parents and therapists can become alternative attachment influences and teach the adolescent that relationships can be caring, safe and nurturing.

Chapter 3

ADULT ATTACHMENT

*S*o now you should have a better understanding of Attachment in childhood and adolescence. The Attachment one develops in childhood typically and logically carries forward into adulthood. Adult Attachments are similar in some ways and different in others. This chapter will help you gain an understanding of Adult Attachment and how it may be relevant to your relationship issues.

Adult Attachments serve the same function as child attachments: to offer comfort, security and safety, particularly during times of stress or illness or injury. Just as children do, we adults want to feel that we have a secure base, with an intimate other to support us, protect us, offer us security and nurturance, particularly when we're feeling stressed or overwhelmed by the demands of life or when we're just not feeling well. Most of us turn to our spouses or partners or good friends when we've had a stressful day. Or certainly we want to do this. Also, if we've had a great day, we want to share the good feeling with someone close to us.

We may think about our partner during the day and find comfort in knowing we have a caring adult in our lives. Similar to children who may find comfort in the day thinking about a loving parent, adults find comfort from the thoughts about their spouse or partner or boyfriend/ girlfriend or someone close to them. If we are far away from our spouses, partners or boyfriends we may look forward to speaking to them on the phone or through social media.

I recall a cartoon in the local newspaper called *Cathy*. It was about a single woman who had a boyfriend that she could never commit to. She did a great work presentation one day and clearly wanted to share the good feeling. The cartoon depicted her coming home to an empty apartment and sharing her joy with her umbrella stand. Although the cartoon tried to make the situation funny, it was actually very sad.

It feels so much more fulfilling to share both our joy and our disappointments with someone close to us.

What is different between adults and children in their attachments is that adults have the capacity to have more than one attachment figure. Whereas infants and young children rely mainly on their primary caregivers, usually parents, adults may have more than one person to turn to for comfort and support. One can have a best friend, a colleague, or a relative, in addition to a spouse or partner with whom one shares their intimate needs and finds comfort in these relationships.

The other significant difference between adult and child attachments is the mutuality of adult attachments. Parents and other caregivers of children may gain pleasure in the relationship with the child but in healthy attachments parents do not expect the child to meet their adult needs for support and nurturing. Parents are the prime caretakers of their children and need to do this without expecting the child to reciprocate by taking care of the parent. Parents have to rely on other adults if they need support and comfort, particularly when parenting becomes taxing and exhausting.

In adult relationships **mutuality** is a significant feature of healthy relationships. At times one partner may have to put aside his or her needs for comfort and support knowing his or her partner is more stressed or upset. At times the other partner will do the same. If each partner believes he or she will get their needs met at another time soon and with enough frequency, each will remain caring and giving in the relationship. If one partner feels they're the one doing most of the giving and not receiving much, over time, the giving partner will feel resentment toward the other. In healthy relationships adults are both caregivers and care receivers in balanced proportions.

For example, one of my clients, Tracy, was a stay at home mother, with two challenging adopted boys. Her husband, Jeff, left for work early and came home at dinner time. Tracy was responsible for the morning routine with the boys and getting them to school. One day, she had a particularly difficult time with the boys who refused to comply with the morning routines. The boys were late for school. They returned home after school and continued to challenge Tracy refusing to do their homework and fighting with each other. Tracy was exhausted and frustrated by the time Jeff came home. She was hoping he would take over the night routine so she could get a break. As soon as Jeff entered the house it was clear that he was irritated and had not had an easy day at work. He greeted the boys but his voice told them he was not in a receptive mood to be playful. He typically was a very involved and loving father.

Jeff briefly told Tracy that there was a major problem at work that was not fully resolved. He was still upset by the issues and would need to spend some time that evening working. Tracy knew she wouldn't be able to share her frustration regarding the boys and receive a sympathetic ear from Jeff. She knew that she would have to find the energy to take care of the boys that evening and let Jeff do his work. She was able to do this knowing that usually she and Jeff cooperated well and supported each other as parents. She was able to put aside her needs for support knowing that Jeff would be available the next day or certainly within a reasonable time. Jeff and Tracy have a secure adult relationship.

This kind of mutuality only works if there is a balance in the give and take in a relationship. If you have the feeling that you are always putting aside your need for support and comfort to take care of your spouse, you will eventually feel resentment. This is true even for people who are caregivers and always want to help. In our close relationships we want to know that we can turn to our spouse/partner when something has gone wrong in our working lives, with our children, with our friends or any other aspect of our lives. We can delay this need for a period of time or one or two times but if we never get this support resentment and anger will set in and eventually damage the relationship.

Adult Attachment Categories

Let's assume you had a troubled childhood with parents that were not available, neglected you or were even abusive to you. You would be an insecure child. Does this mean you would automatically be an insure adult? Not necessarily.

To develop an Insecure Adult Attachment, you would definitely have experienced an insecure early childhood but you would have to experience other kids and other people in your life treating you poorly as well. This often happens because the behaviour of some insecure children is difficult and other people respond negatively.

If you continued to have relationships as an older child and as an adolescent that were troubled and made you feel badly about yourself, you would continue as an adult to perceive yourself as unworthy of loving, nurturing and protective relationships and continue to fear abandonment, rejection, or abuse in relationships. You will have expectations and beliefs that you'll not be treated well in relationships and because of this you'll engage in relationships that are harmful and untrustworthy. Then by choosing an uncaring, unavailable, rejecting or abusive partner your insecurity and expectation about relationships will be confirmed: that your needs for caring, nurturing and safety will not be met in intimate relationships.

My mother came from a neglecting and abusive family in Europe. She came to believe that no one would take care of her and she had to be self-sufficient and independent. She came to Canada as an older adolescent believing her life and relationships would be different. She was sponsored by an aunt and came to live with her aunt and cousins. If they had treated her well and offered her kindness and ongoing support, her belief that she had to be independent and take care of herself may have changed or at least been lessened. But her relatives did not. She had to clean their home, get a job in a factory and help support her extended family. She felt like a slave in that household, not a child who needed encouragement and time to adjust to a new family and country.

My mother's belief that she was alone with no one to care and nurture her was confirmed and this became her way of being in relationships for the rest of her life. She remained fiercely independent with little trust in anyone and little capacity to get close to anyone.

Similar to child attachments there are four classifications of Adult Attachment. These were developed by a researcher in Attachment Theory, Dr. Mary Main, and her associates in 1985. The researchers put together a questionnaire with 15 questions about a person's childhood experiences. The person being interviewed basically tells the story of his or her early childhood. He or she has to describe his or her relationship with parents, give examples or memories to explain why he or she chose those particular adjectives. There are also questions about how one understands the influence of their childhood on their development and understands why their parents raised them as they did. There is a question about one's present relationships with parents.

The person doing the interview has to score the answers, following a manual. This is a research-based way of determining what kind of Adult Attachment a person has.

Determining the classification of Attachment is based on a number of qualities in the interview, including:

- the adjectives and phrases the person being interviewed used to describe his or her relationship with parents or caregivers
- the clarity, consistency, believability and flow of the story of his or her childhood
- the cooperation and motivation to be open and honest with the interviewer
- A person's insight into how his or her childhood affected their present personality and current relationship with their parents.

I don't want you to become overwhelmed by this information or think you have to be interviewed and scored to figure out your Adult Attachment. I will be explaining how you can figure this out by being honest about your behaviour and patterns in relationships. But let me explain a little more about how the interview works to determine one's Adult Attachment. Typically, adults with different types of Attachment will answer the questions differently.

Some people don't give evidence or examples for the descriptions of how their mother or father or other caregivers parented them; some may give too brief a description; others too long a description or go way off topic; and others are very disorganized in describing their childhood story. Some people have an in-depth understanding of the impact of their childhood on their personalities and some have no awareness or deny there was any influence.

I once asked a client of mine to describe his relationship with his mother. He answered: "She was a housewife." I asked if he could tell me more and all he said was that she cooked and cleaned and was a mother. He couldn't tell me anymore nor could he give me any childhood memories of his relationship with his mother.

I had another client who first told me her relationship with mother was wonderful, then added: "Well, she drank and once left me out in the cold." Then she went on to say that her mother was really her grandmother and the woman she thought was her aunt was really her mother. Her mother/grandmother blurted this out when she was drunk and angry. I could barely follow the story of her childhood because it was so confusing and contradictory.

Each of these people have a different Adult Attachment Category. One's interview was too sparse with little information and few memories. The other kept changing her story and was difficult to follow because of the confusing information and memories.

The determination of the Adult Attachment Category isn't based on the absolute accuracy or truth about one's life story. It is more about how you make sense of your early childhood, how you understand how it has impacted on your present personality and relationships and how you relate to your parents as adults. The more you offer a clear and believable childhood story, however lovely or horrible it was, with sympathy for your parents' own life story, the more likely you are to have a Secure Adult Attachment. The more you understand your own strengths and setbacks because of your upbringing, the more likely you are to have a Secure Attachment. So, the type of Adult Attachment you have will be based on the meaning you give to your childhood experiences. This is important to understand.

I will use myself as an example. My mother never understood how her childhood and adolescence left her a mistrustful person who saw the world as an unsafe place. She also instilled this belief about being independent and mistrustful in me. She would say to me: "Never ask anyone for anything because you will then owe them something,"

However, as an adult because of my profession and my own therapy I came to understand how my mother's beliefs impacted me, resulting in my being very independent and self-reliant, not trusting others to be supportive. I understood how these beliefs influenced me both positively and negatively. I realized I had to work at trusting people, at allowing myself to be dependent and vulnerable and at expressing my needs and feelings. I was also able to be much more understanding and empathic to my mother and take care of her in her later years. My acceptance and caretaking of her allowed her to be more dependent and trusting of me. I think her last years were the first time she experienced such caring and nurturance. My security in adulthood allowed us to have this closer relationship.

Secure/Autonomous Attachment

Adults who have had reasonably good parenting—with parents that were caring, loving, understanding and available—develop what is called **Autonomous Attachments**. This is the adult Term for Secure Attachment in Childhood developed by Dr. Main and her associates. Such adults are secure within themselves and value relationships. They expect to be treated well in intimate relationships and believe they can find nurturance, comfort, support and safety in close committed relationships. They usually have a good relationship with their parents as adults and are secure parents for their children.

Adults with Autonomous or Secure Attachments have many positive qualities that enable them to be successful in life. They have both a positive and realistic perception of themselves. They are able to be self-reflective and take responsibility for their own behaviour in relationship problems. They are able to accept that others have different perceptions and try to be non-judgemental and accepting of such differences. Their inner security enables them to be adaptable, resilient and to regulate their emotions.

Earned Security

There is a lovely concept in Attachment Theory, called **Earned Security**. This category is applied to people who had troubled upbringings and because of this should have an Insecure Adult Attachment. But they were able to resolve the negative impact on their personalities and have Secure Attachments as adults. This may be because they had other positive relationships in their lives to compensate for the negative harm of their early childhoods. This may develop because the insecure person went into therapy. In therapy that insecure adult would have examined his or her early childhood experiences, understood the impact of these experiences on his or her adult development and established a trusting relationship with a therapist. The therapeutic experience would have enabled the adult to explore and understand why their parents parented the way they did and perhaps forgive their parents knowing they had their own poor childhood experiences.

This understanding and the trust with the therapist can change how an insecure person sees herself or himself and can also change his or her expectations about relationships. Earned Secure people move internally from feeling negative about themselves to feeling positive and move externally from choosing harmful partners to choosing helpful partners.

They develop "Earned Security."

When Marjorie became a young adult, after a childhood of abuse, she was very insecure. She had not dated as an adolescent for fear of boys hurting her but more because she feared anyone getting close to her. She believed they would discover how dirty and bad she was, having been sexually abused. There was a young man at her place of work that she noticed. He was always neatly dressed, smelled so clean and was polite to everyone. When he asked her out Marjorie accepted although she was terrified. His name was Allen. On the first date Marjorie noticed his hands were small, clean and well-manicured, nothing like those of her father. In fact nothing about Allen was similar to her father. Marjorie continued to date Allen until she was convinced he looked and acted nothing like her father. It was this reality that enabled Marjorie to marry Allen.

Marjorie was correct in her assessment of Allen. He was a kind, patient, loving and protective man. He knew nothing about Marjorie's' abuse but realized she was a very naive insecure young woman who needed his protection. And he did protect her throughout their married life.

Because of her relationship with Allen, Marjorie did become more secure and could function better in her life. She remained unresolved about her trauma until later in her life when she went into therapy with me. This therapy helped Marjorie understand the impact of the abuse on her development and to place responsibility for the abuse on her father, not herself. She came to understand that her father had been traumatized by his war experiences. This didn't excuse the abuse he perpetrated on Marjorie but gave her a different perspective on his behaviour.

As Marjorie resolved her trauma a more secure person emerged that could honour her potential. Marjorie was a very talented and creative person whose potential had been crushed She hadn't been able to concentrate in school anticipating abuse when she went home. She was streamed into vocational studies because the school personnel perceived her as cognitively slow. They were wrong. By the time Marjorie completed her therapy, she was drawing, painting and writing with growing assurance and talent.

The relationship with her husband and her therapeutic relationship with me enabled Marjorie to develop Earned Security in her later years. This positive perception of herself and greater trust in relationships allowed Marjorie to be more open with her husband and her adult children about her abuse and take greater risks in her own self-development.

Insecure Preoccupied (Anxious-Ambivalent)

Children who had Anxious Ambivalent Attachments grow up to have Insecure Preoccupied Attachments. As explained in Chapter 2, these were children who had caregivers who were inconsistently available. Such children were always hyper-vigilant about a caregiver not being available and came to believe they had to demand attention with intense feelings and manipulate their caregivers to get their needs met. As adults they remain very insecure dependent people who look for someone to offer them stability, constant reassurance and availability and for someone to complete them.

They become preoccupied with the whereabouts of their partners when they're not available, even for legitimate reasons. This preoccupation with the availability of their partner becomes self-defeating because they alienate their partner with their dependency, possessiveness, constant demand for attention and reassurance. Such feelings are expressed with intense affect. They can fluctuate from extreme anger to regret, to sadness and charm and back to anger in what feels to their partner as a wild cycle. They're jealous of any relationships their partners have, even legitimate working relationships. They can be very difficult in relationships because of the push / pull effect that their anger and seductive charm causes. They push their partner away with their anger, get scared by the distance and then use charm, seduction and even fake illness to pull their partners back into being close.

Preoccupied people tend to devalue themselves and overvalue their partners particularly in the beginning of the relationship. The idealization of the partner may change in the relationship as they experience their partners as unavailable or insensitive to their dependency needs. Then their anger and resentment takes over.

Even as adults they may continue to have conflict with their parents, still longing for their parents to meet their needs.

When Mindy first met her husband, Cliff, she thought he was perfect. She couldn't believe that he was interested in her. She was certainly not as smart, attractive, fit or successful as him. Cliff pursued her and on every date he would organize their activities and made her feel loved and cherished. She developed a dependency on him and continued to think he was a perfect man.

After they got married this idealized man changed. He worked long hours, worked out at the gym every day and became more critical of her. Mindy found herself becoming angry at him and frightened that he wasn't the man she married. She would call him at work when she could and was upset that he didn't call her back. When she came home and he didn't return until much later in the evening, she would wait for him seething inside. Initially he would apologize, be affectionate to her, and ensure they ate and spent time together. Gradually even these intimate gestures lessened.

Initially Mindy complained to Cliff that she needed and wanted him home more. He would say he had to work late because he had meetings and was building the business for them. He invited her to join him at the gym. When Cliff didn't change his behaviour, Mindy began to complain louder until one day she became furious at Cliff, called him foul names, threw something at him, tried to hit him and eventually broke down sobbing. Cliff held her, re-assured her that he loved her and promised he would try and be more available. But as Mindy's behaviour became more aggressive and out of control, Cliff became more distant, telling Mindy she was crazy and had to see a psychiatrist. Mindy began to feel she was crazy and wondered what happened to the wonderful man she married and the happiness she had felt when they were dating.

Mindy had an insecure Preoccupied Attachment and married a man who was Dismissing, confirming for her no one was consistently available and activating her feelings of anxiety and anger.

Insecure Dismissing (Avoidant)

The child who had parents who were unavailable or rejecting learned to avoid them. The child who figured out that closeness to parents was based on being the perfect child or taking care of a selfish parent becomes an adult who find closeness very difficult. These are adults who are more comfortable working hard, involving in activities and showing love through material goods. They have great difficulty expressing feelings, being empathic and enjoying intimate passive moments. They tend to push away or deactivate their needs for closeness in relationships. Their spouses and partners experience such adults as cold, detached, unaffectionate, emotionally unavailable but responsible and successful. They're adults with **Dismissing Attachments**.

Dismissing Attached adults may present a superior sense of self and may be high functioning and successful in careers and activities. Their independence and self-sufficiency is based on the belief that they have to take care themselves and not rely on anyone else. They're often unaware of their feelings and if they have a sense of their feelings, they're unable to express this. They often prefer to be alone or more involved in work and extracurricular activities than in close relationships. We all know of workaholics who devote more time and energy to their jobs and professions than to their families and marriages. The workaholic is an example of a Dismissing Attached person. If Dismissing Attached adults are involved in social relationships, these are often superficial, and based on activities, drinking and group relationships. They wouldn't turn to such relationships for comfort or support.

Some children had parents who were somewhat loving if the child was well behaved, did well in school and extracurricular activities and grew up to be successful. As adults such children would continue to believe that, if they were good people, hardworking and provided well for their families, they would be loved. They're genuinely puzzled when their spouses/partners complain that they're not emotionally available. They expect their partners to be loving and to value them since they're good caretakers and providers. This is what they learned as children. They're adults with Dismissing Attachments of a certain type.

Brian and Joyce were both accountants when they married. Both were hard working and successful in their careers. Joyce was attracted to Brian because he was intelligent, conscientious and ambitious. She knew he would provide well for her and the children they planned to have. When Joyce got pregnant she and Brian agreed she would stay home and look after the child and any other children until they were in school.

Joyce found herself very alone as the primary caregiver to two children. Brian worked late almost every night and even weekends. When he was home their relationship focused on the tasks around the house. As their children grew, he became active in their sports. He demanded that Joyce be on a strict budget although he earned a high salary. Joyce became angrier and angrier at the man she married. She felt she had given up her career for him. He seemed to be available to her only to do work around the house and for sexual pleasure.

When she complained to Brian that she didn't feel any emotional closeness with him he said it was because she was cold and rejecting and didn't work with him on their finances. He also became angry, at times yelling at her. Joyce threatened to leave if they didn't go into marital therapy.

In their therapy I explored with Brian how he was feeling about his wife's complaints. He looked at me as if I was speaking a foreign language. He said: "What do you mean?" I explained that I was referring to feelings such as anger, sadness, fear, which would all be valid given the problems in their marriage. Brian continued to be puzzled saying he didn't know how he felt.

In exploring Brian's history, he described feeling loved by his parents although they never said "I love you" or demonstrate any affection or love. He felt most valued by his parents when he did well at school or was good in his extracurricular activities. He knew receiving higher education, excelling at University, and having a career was expected of him. His parents also expected him to be mindful of his spending and always have savings. He gained success, always feeling superior to his peers that were not successful. He felt his success made his parents proud and this was very important to him. He dated in University and had some friends but this was secondary to his academic pursuits. He secured a job with a good accounting firm as soon as he graduated. He knew one day he would be a partner. He told me that he had a good relationship with his parents who lived in another province but acknowledged he had little contact with them and visited them infrequently.

Brian is an excellent example of a person with a Dismissing Attachment. He learned to push away any of his feelings as a child, particularly vulnerable feelings, and came to believe he had to achieve and be independent to get his parents' approval. He was a very good boy but at the expense of his feelings of needing others or any feelings of vulnerability, sadness, even joy. This inability to be emotionally close came to haunt him in his marriage and as a parent.

Unresolved (Disorganized) Attachments

Children who have traumatic childhood experiences continue to see the world and relationships as dangerous if they haven't resolved the trauma. Such trauma can include physical, emotional or sexual abuse, extreme neglect, being victims of violence or witnessing violence. Trauma can also be the result of the early loss of a primary caregiver that the child hasn't mourned. Without the resolution of the trauma or loss in childhood such children become adults with **Unresolved Attachments**.

As adults they continue to use the strategies they developed as children to protect themselves. They may use aggression, avoidance or fleeing from people and situations or shut down completely. They can become victims in relationships or offenders. They're easily triggered by experiences in their daily lives and may have distortions about people and situations based on their perception that people are unsafe. Adults who experienced extreme trauma may present with dissociative behaviour which means that they remove themselves psychologically from their present situation. It's as if they are day dreaming but can't come back to reality. They usually learned to do this as children to remove themselves from the frightening person or situation. They have great difficulty in intimate relationships since they're often triggered by closeness with others.

Let's consider Marjorie again who remained unresolved about her childhood traumatic experiences until late in her adult life. She had been sexually abused by her father but he also terrorized the family by yelling and belittling everyone, including Marjorie's mother and brothers. She avoided closeness by being a sweet considerate person who always deflected attention away from herself. She learned to ask others about themselves and so ensured no one learned anything about her. In her therapy, she would ask how I was doing, how my daughter and son were doing and would ask about anything else she could remember about me. In time Marjorie and I could laugh about this avoidance, but she also did this with everyone else.

Marjorie profoundly believed that she was defective and would contaminate others if they got close. She was able to work, be a wife and mother but always felt fragile and inadequate. Marjorie had a full-blown traumatic response one day when a supervisor at work raised her voice at Marjorie. Marjorie left work that day and never returned. She stayed in bed hidden under the covers and couldn't leave her room. Eventually her husband forced her to see their family doctor who put Marjorie on anti-depressants. He wrote a letter for her employer and Marjorie went on disability. She didn't understand what happened to her nor did she ever work again. She didn't realize that the loud voice of her supervisor had reminded her of the rage of her father and sent her spinning into a traumatic state. This experience left her feeling inadequate, shamed, terrorized and helpless.

Having More Than One Attachment Category

Typically, a person has a primary Attachment Category but can have one or more secondary Attachments. The main attachment category develops from the interaction with the caregiver who has been the primary attachment figure. One can develop a secondary attachment if a child has another parent or involved caregiver, such as a grandmother, who is significantly involved in the upbringing. A child whose parents divorced early in their childhood can develop a significant secondary attachment if that child was equally involved with each parent from an early age. With fathers more significantly involved from infancy and more gay and lesbian parents sharing parenting, secondary attachments may be more common. Since the brain of an infant can only internalize one attachment figure in the first six months, the parent or caregiver most available in the first year will be the primary attachment figure.

Carol, a client of mine, is a good example of someone who has one primary Attachment but also has a secondary attachment that influences her responses in close relationships. Carol's mother was a narcissistic woman who needed her children to always look good and perform well so she would look good to the external world. She would sew clothes for the children, make dolls, be active in the community but Carol felt it was always in the service of impressing everyone with her talents, not to meet the needs of her children. In fact she would tell Carol and her siblings that she wished she'd never had children. At times she would threaten to leave. Carol felt that she had to be the perfect child to engage her mother. Since she wasn't a perfect child, Carol always felt that she wasn't good enough and was a burden.

Carol idealized her father. She felt he was a supportive figure in her life who tried to compensate for the gap her mother created. He did much of the housekeeping chores and was supportive and protective of his children. She experienced him as giving her priority in his life and knew she could always rely on him being available. He was supportive of the relationship between Carol and her mother valuing the integrity of the family and believing in the importance of the mother/child relationships. Although Carol tended to idealize her father and one could question how valid her perception was, she did experience him as loving and available.

Carol also had a grandmother who was very involved in Carol's life and was the primary caregiver at lunch time and after school. Carol felt close to her and would go to her if she was sick or upset. Her grandmother would hold her and rock her and tell her she'd be fine.

Carol's primary Attachment is Insecure Dismissing. She continued to believe as an adult that she had to be perfect and focused on doing well at school and University and being self-disciplined. She tended to isolate herself and just focus on being the perfect student and professional. She tended to try and be what other people wanted in intimate relationships and to take care of their needs. She engaged in destructive relationships with men who couldn't meet her needs. She described not even knowing what she wanted or needed and being able to detach from her feelings.

Yet, Carol valued relationships and continued as an adult to value the relationship with her father. Her parents separated when Carol was an adult. Carol moved to another city and physically and emotionally distanced herself from her mother. She continued to have a close relationship with her father, communicating regularly with him and feeling his concern and interest in her. She knew that she was loved unconditionally by her father and felt some sense of self-worth through this relationship. Her grandmother had died when Carol was a teenager but Carol had internalized this caring and nurturing relationship. Because of her attachment to the other two adults in her life, Carol's secondary attachment was Secure Autonomous.

Although her relationship with her daughter and male partners was problematic, Carol valued these relationships and worked at improving them. She willingly entered therapy recognizing her problems in these relationships and her need to understand herself better, particularly to improve her relationship with her daughter.

Chapter 4

DETERMINING YOUR OWN
ATTACHMENT CLASSIFICATION

Why is it important and useful to understand your own Attachment
Type? Having some knowledge about your Attachment may
help you understand yourself and particularly why you have chosen the
partner or partners you have and why you behave the way you do in close
relationships. Understanding yourself from an Attachment perspective
should help you be less critical and angry at yourself for these choices
and your behaviour. Attachment theory explains that your negative
view of yourself that leads to problematic choices comes from your
childhood experiences, which you couldn't control as a child. Sadly, those
experiences continue to influence you as an adult.

Many of us consciously tell ourselves that we will not choose someone
like our cold and unaffectionate mother or like our abusive father. And we
think we have. Then we learn that the person we married or partnered
with is just like that parent. Your unconscious internalized model of
relationships dominated your choice. This unconscious drive was more
powerful than your conscious determination to choose differently.

But I want to assure you that as an adult with awareness of your Attachment Category and the will to change you can create new and healthier
patterns in intimate relationships.

How do you determine your Attachment Type? You can have a formal Adult Attachment Assessment done by someone trained to do this. But this process is costly and there are few therapists trained to conduct and score the interview. There are questionnaires that ask directly how you feel about your partner and how you behave in that relationship. You can get an impression of your Attachment Type by examining the descriptions of the different classifications and being honest with yourself about which description applies to you.

I gave a general description of the different Attachment Classifications in the previous chapter. The following are the classifications in a more detailed form. The descriptions include the different qualities of parenting or caregiving you may have experienced as a young child and then the descriptions of behaviour and attitudes that apply to each Attachment Category. Read each one carefully and apply whatever descriptions ring true for you. Write them down. You may find that descriptions from more than one category apply to you.

I am going to use the combination of child and adult attachments categories when I am describing adult attachments. This will make it easier for you to understand that a particular child attachment develops into an Adult Attachment Category.

By thinking about yourself, remembering how you were parented in early childhood and reflecting on both your past and who you are now, you'll begin to understand your Attachment Category and perhaps start the process of change.

Secure/Autonomous Attachment

People with Secure/Autonomous Adult Attachments can usually describe their childhood experiences with ease and openness and have lots of memories. So, if you had a secure upbringing and were telling this to a friend or someone interviewing you this is what your story would sound like:

- If you were to describe your relationship with your primary caregiver, particularly your mother, you would say that she or he was loving, available, fun, affectionate and supportive during times of illness, hurt or stress.
- You would be able to access childhood memories that substantiate the above descriptions. You could describe these memories to someone with enough detail, easy flow and openness that they are believable and sound. You may want to try and do this.

The descriptions below are other qualities that Autonomous/Secure Adults have in themselves or demonstrate in relationships:

- You value relationships and believe that having a close intimate other is important in your life.
- You ensure you have time for relationships and turn to intimate others both when you want to share happy experiences and when you need support and care because you are stressed or sad about events in your life.
- You are also comfortable to be independent and alone. You like yourself, have confidence in your abilities and personal qualities and enjoy doing some activities on your own.
- You are able to accept easily when your spouse, partner or children separate from you and have other important relationships in their lives.
- When you do have problems in relationships you examine and accept your part in such problems. You are able to reflect on yourself, accept your mistakes, learn from them and change your behaviour.
- You believe that you will be able to resolve problems in relationships and do not worry that the relationship is threatened by conflict and will terminate.
- This ability to accept yourself also allows you to be accepting of the differences in others.

- You are able to express your needs, wants and feelings in relationships in an emotionally balanced way.
- You are able to be sympathetic, empathic and understanding of the needs and feelings of others.

You're a well-balanced person that others want to have as a friend or partner. You're probably successful in your career, in your parenting and in your close relationships. You usually feel good about yourself. You feel secure.

Earned Security

Earned Security is a concept developed by Mary Main and Associates[1] to explain why some people who describe terrible family histories score as Secure on the Adult Attachment Interview or present as secure in relationships as described by the above description. This category is very hopeful for those individuals who were raised in an insecure parenting environment. How does one overcome such detriments and develop into a secure adult. This can occur for a number of reasons:

- A child may have alternative attachment figures in their life. This can be the parent of a friend who the child sees often and who treats the child in a caring and loving manner. It can be a teacher who may know about a child's difficult life and offer them much support and nurturing. Teachers see children on a daily basis for at least a school term so can play the role of an Attachment Figure. A child may have a relative, like a grandparent, who is loving and caring and whom the child sees often. Alternative Attachment figures have to see a child with enough intensity and frequency to influence a child. Children will take

---

1 Hesse, Erik, The Adult Attachment Interview, in Cassidy, Jude &Shaver, Phillip, Handbook of Attachment, 1999, Guilford Press, New York, p.401

in positive experiences with another adult and come to believe that they are lovable and worthy only if they spend lots of time with that adult.

- An adolescent may come to recognize that their parent or parents are not consistently caring adults, not available much of the time or abusive and neglectful. Because the adolescent brain is rapidly changing, particularly the thinking and analyzing section of the brain, adolescents have a greater capacity to think about their family situation. Because peers become more important as attachment figures the adolescent may seek out peers that are supportive. A boyfriend or girlfriend may understand the background of the adolescent they are partnered with and hang in even during difficult times. An adolescent may experience a friend or the parents of a friend as so caring and empathic he or she may come to believe that other people are not like their parents and come to trust close relationships.

- An adult may also choose a partner or spouse who offers him or her a nurturing unconditional loving experience that changes his/her negative belief about relationships and their perception of herself or himself. This may occur because of luck, circumstances or because one is determined not to partner or marry someone like their parent.

- A child, adolescent or adult may enter therapy and develop a relationship with a therapist that is caring, nurturing, and supportive. In time this relationship changes the old negative Internal Model of Relationships to one that is positive, involving trust and security in relationships. Adolescents and Adults are most able to use a therapeutic relationship to examine their early childhood experiences, come to understand the impact on their personalities, begin to risk being more open and trusting in the therapeutic relationship and eventually transfer this to their "real life" relationships.

Typically, people with Earned Security have come to understand that their childhood experiences created significant setbacks for them in relationships but also life successes. They may understand why their parents parented them so poorly and may have forgiven them. They've used this insight to make changes in their patterns in relationships and come to perceive themselves as valuable and worthy of caring and success in their lives. Thus they have earned their security.

Gregory was a child that I worked with in therapy for many years. He was adopted by older parents when he was four years old. He arrived with many problems. His adoptive mother only felt the desire for children in her forties after she resolved issues with her own mother. Unfortunately for Gregory his mother became ill in his first year of being adopted and died in his second year. Gregory was left with a detached father who had been ambivalent about the adoption from the beginning. Gregory was diagnosed with a Reactive Attachment Disorder and went into therapy soon after being adopted. He was aggressive, defiant of authority, had poor peer relationships and could not perform academically.

Eventually Gregory received Attachment Focused Therapy with me which involved his father and was placed in a special education class. In time he came to trust his teacher and me. He also came to believe that his father was committed to him although limited in his capacity for expressing any feelings of love or nurturing. By adolescence Gregory was more regulated emotionally, doing somewhat better in school and had developed close and trustworthy peer relationships. By older adolescence he had a long term romantic relationship that he valued and in which he could express his feelings of love and respect.

As a young adult Gregory was living on his own, had accepted the emotional limitations of his father and valued the financial support he offered. Gregory had developed his creative talents and was trying to pursue a career in this area. He had a few close friends, acquired a pet and had a job he was excited about. He continued to be in contact with me, using me as a support and confidant in times of need. His long-standing girlfriend had ended the relationship. He reported that he was heart-broken for a time but understood that this was part of his life experience. He could express his fears about entering into another romantic relationship but recognized the importance of risking this one day.

Although Gregory hadn't focused on and resolved his early experience in the orphanage, he had mourned the loss of the mother he longed for and had a realistic and non-judgemental acceptance of his father. I believe the relationships he had with me, his therapist, and his teacher, which lasted for years, helped him feel valued and loved unconditionally. This perception of himself as lovable enabled him to develop healthy peer relationships and accept having a limited relationship with his father. Gregory had developed enough Earned Security to be more successful in relationships and in his job.

Preoccupied-Anxious Attachments

To determine if you fit into this category, check to see if the following descriptions apply to you:

- If you were describing your family history to a therapist, it would be in a confusing and rambling manner. You would describe your mother or primary caregiver as sometimes wonderful and involved with you and sometimes angry and rejecting of you. You could not predict which mood she would have, but you were always checking on this. You might describe feeling anxious and angry at your mother.
- As an adult you still have this feeling of anxiety and insecurity. You feel a desperate need for relationships and are dependent on others for your security and self-worth.

- Because of the inconsistency by your parent you are very vigilant about the availability of any partner and are easily triggered into feelings of jealousy and insecurity. You think about your partner/spouse a great deal of your time away from him or her. These insecure feelings may lead you to accuse your partner/spouse of having affairs or caring about his/her colleagues and other people more than you. You may start to check on his/her whereabouts or check his/her emails and messages. This desperate and demanding behaviour may push away the person or people you care about. Even knowing this often does not help you stop your desperate behaviour.

- You have great difficulty controlling your feelings. Whether you are feeling anger, sadness, fear, anxiety or joy you experience these with great intensity. You may have learned in childhood that if you express your needs with intensity, such as having temper tantrums, your parent would pay attention to you. You may continue to believe this but now you are an adult and expressing anxiety and anger with great force usually alienates people, does not bring them closer.

- You have great difficulty being independent, making independent decisions and trusting your judgement. You rely on others to direct you but may need the opinions of many others, which in the end is confusing and leaves you helpless to make any decision.

- You tend to overvalue your partner or spouse, particularly in the beginning of a relationship and devalue yourself. You do not understand why the person has chosen you yet you become involved very quickly. Your intense feelings and immediate dependency may drive the person away.

Sonia came to me as an older woman who was having great difficulty in her long-term marriage. The husband she had idealized was no longer behaving wonderfully and she was struggling with what to do about her marriage. She was angry at her husband, anxious about his lack of interest in her but completely dependent on him. Sonia described her early childhood as wonderful but acknowledged that she was always with her parents and never encouraged to be independent. She was very close to her mother who could be both very loving but also angry and demanding. Her parents had experienced severe trauma in their lives and so felt the need to be overprotective of their daughter.

When Sonia met Peter, the man who would become her husband, she fell head over heels in love. She thought he was perfect. He was outgoing, charming, successful and had many friends. Sonia was shy, more bookish and had very few friends. She became totally preoccupied with Peter, secretly following him.

Eventually, Peter asked Sonia to marry him. Her parents were not thrilled with Peter. He wasn't of their faith and culture, but he assured Sonia's father that he would take care of her and provide a good life for her. Sonia married Peter, believing she'd found the perfect man. She entered into his world, becoming part of his social life, taking on his interests and helping him in business. She helped create the image of a perfect family life, where her husband and children looked good, where the house in which they lived was spectacular, where she made her husband feel that whatever he took on he did flawlessly. Sonia's sense of self was completely tied to the life style and personality of her husband. When her mother died, Sonia needed her husband more and soon became more aware of his unavailability. She began noticing his attentiveness to others and his preference for his activities over her. She began to feel anger and expressed this with intense feelings and actions, until on one day she lost it and threw something at her husband in front of their friends.

The relationship deteriorated but Sonia couldn't let go of this idealized man and remained preoccupied with him long after the marriage ended.

Dismissing/Avoidant Attachments

You will be considered a Dismissing/avoidant Attachment if you fit the following description:

- You describe a childhood history of neglect or rejection or conditional love but deny the importance of this on your personality development. You may say things like "that happened a long time ago and has nothing to do with my life now"

- You may idealize your parents but cannot give any memories or examples of what they did that justify the idealized adjectives. For example, you may say your mother was a great mother but cannot describe in any detail what she did that was loving or nurturing.

- You may not be able to give any description or a very sparse description of your parents or your early childhood experience saying you do not remember.

- You value your independence and prefer to be self-sufficient and not be dependent on others. It is difficult for you to ask for help or turn to others for support if you allow yourself to feel vulnerable.

- You tend to suppress feelings of vulnerability, sadness or fear. You may allow feelings of anger but rarely recognize that underlying the anger are unmet needs.

- Your needs go unmet because it is so difficult for you to express your needs in close relationships. Expressing needs can make one feel dependent and this is too frightening for you.

- You prefer to involve in activities than in close relationships. You may be a workaholic, involved in sports and other extracurricular activities and prefer to do activities with people rather than talk and share feelings.

- You ensure that you keep your distance from people that you suspect may reject you or whom you consider superior to you.

- You may view yourself as superior or present this image to others

- You may be very successful in your career, chosen activities or in superficial relationships but find your partner, spouse, girlfriend/boyfriends complaining you are emotionally distant.

Raymond is a client I had who would fit this description. He came to see me because he was feeling detached from his wife and generally wasn't in touch with feelings. When I asked him to describe his relationship with his mother, he said she was a housewife. He could not elaborate or give me any other description. He described his father as never home and not involved with his children. His parents seemed very uninvolved with their son. He described being in love with a girlfriend in university. He had no need to see her frequently nor did he miss her when she attended another university. He would visit her on occasion and felt his limited contact was indicative of his commitment to her. He was shocked when she terminated the relationship telling him that she felt rejected by him and didn't feel he loved her. He missed her after the relationship ended but didn't make any effort to tell her and reconcile with her.

Raymond was very successful in his career and very active in sports. He didn't look forward to going home to his wife and felt no emotional connection to her. He had moved far away from his parents and had very little contact with them. He didn't have any close friends.

Raymond would be categorized as a Dismissing Adult Attachment. He appeared well functioning, was successful in his career and devoted much of his extra time to sports and superficial social activities. He avoided close relationships all of his adult life, was out of touch with his feelings and didn't feel any intimacy with his wife.

Unresolved/Disorganized Attachments

As I mentioned earlier people with Unresolved Attachments have usually suffered some trauma or significant loss in their lives which remains unresolved and affects the present. If you have an Unresolved Attachment, you will demonstrate the following patterns:

- You may describe a confusing family history, sometimes speaking in the past, sometimes talking as if the past was still present and sometimes avoiding talking about your history because it is too painful to remember. You may not remember much of your early family history if you suffered significant trauma.
- You are easily triggered by many events, situations, sensory stimulants like taste, touch, smell and sounds.
- Being triggered means you react to a situation, person, event or sensory stimulant in an extreme way that is not appropriate to what happened or what you experienced, emotionally or with your senses, such as smelling, touching, hearing or eating something.
- You may find yourself becoming disoriented during difficult discussions or situations and not sure what is happening to you.
- You may disconnect emotionally and psychologically so you feel you are not present in the moment and not relating to the people in your life.
- You may find that you cannot control your emotions and moods and find that your moods change without apparent cause or warning.
- Such changes in moods may be frightening to your children or your spouse/partner, yet you cannot control them.
- You may be unable to sleep well at night because of the intrusion of memories of the trauma, or because you have disturbing dreams or nightmares.
- You cannot concentrate also because of intrusive thoughts and memories.

- Sexual intimacy may be difficult for you because of the reminders of earlier abuse.
- In extreme cases a person may not remember what they did or where they were for a day or sometimes days.
- In very extreme and rare cases a person may feel he or she has more than one personality which emerges at different times.

You may discover that more than one description applies to your personality or behaviour. As I mentioned, usually a person has one primary attachment category but may have one or two sub categories.

An example of this is Carrie, a client I worked with who had a mother that was inconsistently available so as a child my client described feeling anxious and angry at her mother. At times she would be defiant and non-compliant but then would feel that her mother was becoming very distant. This distance would scare Carrie so she'd find ways to pull her mother back into a closer relationship. She'd become sweet and well-behaved, doing everything to please her mother. This child had a grandmother who lived nearby and who was loving and nurturing. My client described always trusting that she could go to her grandmother when her mother was angry and rejecting.

This client had great difficulty trusting in her relationship with her partner and was very sensitive to his unavailability. If he worked late or involved with other people, she'd become very jealous and angry. She'd check his phone and emails convinced he was involved with another woman. She'd become preoccupied with this, thinking over and over again that he didn't love her and was seeing someone else. She'd confront him with her suspicions, with intense emotions. She'd become angry, cry, and then beg for reassurance. This aspect of her personality and her emotional behaviour reflected her Preoccupied Attachment state of mind.

She could also be reassured by her partner that he loved her and was committed to her. With this reassurance she could calm down, believe her partner's words, could self-reflect and reason with herself that her intense reaction was her insecurity. In her calmer state she had a realistic perception of her partner and knew he was a reliable and trustworthy man. This aspect of herself emerged from her sense of security and autonomy internalized from the relationship with her grandmother. She couldn't always capture this more secure feeling but it was available to her when her husband was able to be the secure reassuring attachment figure she needed.

Chapter 5

ADULT ATTACHMENT
AND YOUR BRAIN

W hen a baby is growing in its mother's stomach it is not attaching in the way we're discussing. A mother who wanted to get pregnant will get pleasure out of being pregnant, for the most part, and will ensure she eats properly, takes care of her health and the health of the foetus growing inside her. She'll visit a doctor regularly to monitor her baby's development and plan for the birth. The infant growing inside her is completely unaware of this. Its job is purely biological—to develop all its bodily parts and its neurological potential as nature and its genetic makeup intended.

What about mothers who didn't want to get pregnant or were in terrible stressful relationships or circumstances during their pregnancy? There's some evidence that, if a mother had a high anxiety level or was extremely depressed during her pregnancy, this may affect the baby's cognitive and chemical development at birth. This would occur because the mother would have a high level of Cortisol, the stress hormone which can pass through the placenta.[2]

---

2 Zeindler, Christine, Prenatal Maternal Stress, Douglas Mental Health University Institute, Jan, 2013 (online article)

But there is also evidence that the placenta can protect the foetus, even from street drugs and alcohol that a mother took during her pregnancy. Some babies are affected neurologically from the drugs and alcohol and some are not. Some women seem to have more protective placentas, so the baby doesn't become addicted to the drugs or develop brain problems from the alcohol. More research needs to be done to understand better how the foetus is affected by maternal prenatal stress, depression and drug use.

I had a mother whose son I had seen in therapy. He had serious psychotic symptoms and the mother wondered if this was because she'd been in a stressful situation when she was pregnant. She always felt guilty about this. I assured her that this was probably not the case and that his psychosis was probably genetically based although there was no known history of psychosis in his family. Schizophrenia and other psychotic disorders are now believed to be genetically based or certainly a brain irregularity. They are not Attachment Disorders.

The majority of babies are born with the potential for Secure Attachment. We know that some babies are neurologically compromised because of genetic limitations and other inexplicable reasons. Babies who are cognitively impaired, have autism, have Down's Syndrome or other disorders may have limitations in their natural ability to form normal healthy attachments. Babies born to mothers who used drugs and/or alcohol during pregnancy may also be damaged in their attachment potential.

In this chapter and book, I am describing how attachment develops in babies born with what we consider normal brain structures and normal neurological potential.

Understanding how your brain develops will help you understand how Attachment develops, how it is deeply imbedded in the brain at an unconscious or unaware level, why you choose the partner or partners you do and why changing your Attachment Pattern as an adult is challenging but possible.

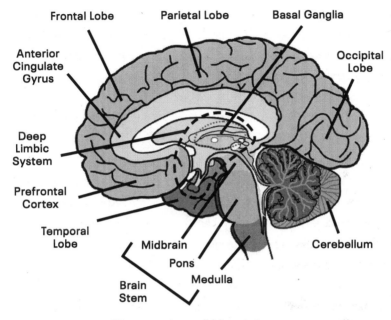

Humananatomyall.blogspot.com

There are three main parts to the brain, each different in structure, function and chemistry. (See above diagram of brain.) Each component of the brain is built on the foundation of the previous structure. The experiences an infant and child has in his or her early years act as the primary builders of the brain's formation and structure. How the brain forms in these early years, based on the child's experience with its caregivers, will influence the brain's capacities in many areas for life. These early relationships become imprinted on the brain and act as templates or models for all other relationships throughout the life of the child. It means that how children are parented or taken care of as babies is so very important to how they will value themselves and the people they'll chose as close friends and partners.

The most primitive part of the brain is called the Brain Stem or the Reptilian Brain. This is the part of our brain that regulates automatic behaviours such as sleeping, breathing, heart rate, blinking and hunger. You're probably breathing as you read this, blinking and maybe feeling pangs of hunger. This is your Brain Stem doing its job without you having to think about it. It is also the part of our brain that is tuned to danger and responds with instinctive protective strategies. This is the part of your brain that will experience fear if you hear a noise in your house you don't recognize. Or when a not so friendly stranger comes up to your baby and you feel immediately protective. You're not thinking; you're reacting instinctively.

When an infant is born this is the part of the brain that is functioning and requires a predictive, regulated and calm environment. Infants at this phase of development need to have healthy sleeping and eating patterns, need a caregiver who figures out what a baby's cries communicate and offers empathic and nurturing responses. Some Mothers, including me, feel that in the first few months, all babies need is to sleep, eat, pee and poo. These are the needs of the primitive brain, but babies need to feel that caregivers understand this and respond to these needs with love, caring, predictability and pleasure. Babies who are raised in the very early years in a nurturing, calm and predictable environment will have brain stems that are optimally functioning. Such well-developed brain structures allow the infant and later the child and adult to be calm and emotionally regulated.

Even babies who are born with brain "wiring" that makes them more cranky and harder to settle, will become more stable and self-controlled if they have mothers or caregivers who remain calm and patient in response to their infant's irritable and seemingly uncontrollable behaviour.

For instance, some of you may have had a "colicky" baby who went through a period of inconsolable crying. You may have tried various methods of soothing your baby without success. Some of you may have become very frustrated and angry at your baby for making your life so miserable. Your anger may have contributed to your baby's upset or certainly wouldn't have helped your baby find whatever comfort she or he could in your arms.

Hopefully many of you managed to stay calm and sympathetic to the discomfort your baby was experiencing. You may have been exhausted and wished your baby would settle, but you didn't personalize your baby's crying or get angry. By remaining calm and empathic to your baby with your soothing sounds and movements, you helped your baby feel comforted even if he or she was still having physical pain.

I recall a colicky phase my daughter went through as an infant. By recognizing she was having stomach pain and by my staying calm I was able to try a number of interventions. Even when none of them seemed to help her, I kept trying. I understood that my daughter was truly having a difficult physical time and not trying to make me feel helpless, although I was having such feelings. As I mentioned previously, I eventually discovered that, by rocking her in an up and down motion by bending and standing I could ease her discomfort and she could sleep.

Staying calm as a parent, not personalizing your baby's dysregulation, helps your infant's developing brain become organized and be the best it can be. By focusing on your baby's need for comfort and not getting angry and frustrated, your infant's brain chemistry will become balanced.

We know that babies who are born constitutionally easy and regulated don't remain easy and happy babies if their caregivers are unpredictable, disorganized or frightening. When babies and children are raised in environments where they are neglected, threatened and abused, their brain chemistry is out of whack and their brain remains stuck at a primitive developmental state. They often have increased anxiety, startle responses and sleep and eating abnormalities. They don't develop basic trust in the people who are supposed to take care of them. These are the people who scare and hurt or neglect them.

The part of the brain that is more relevant to Attachment is the **limbic system** or the emotional brain. This part of the brain is slower to mature and develops based on the experience the baby and child is having in its environment. A child's limbic system's neurological connections need considerable emotional, social, and cognitive stimulation during the first several months and years of life to develop normally. These connections provide the foundations for the child's emotional and social connections and behaviour for life. This is the part of the brain that's the foundation for Attachment.

The limbic system holds the capacity for remembering and internalizing the interactions that occur between an infant and mother or caregiver in the early years. The infant's memory and internalization of the relationship between the infant and caregiver is stored in a particular part of the limbic system called the amygdala. It is stored there at an unconscious level. The child cannot describe in words what he or she remembers as a baby nor describe as a young child the relationships she or he has with his or her parent or caregiver. Yet this memory and that early relationship act as a template for relationships and continue to operate throughout the lifetime of the child, at this unaware level.

For instance, a baby who sees its mother's face while breast feeding and sees its mother smile and look lovingly at him or her will remember this at an emotional level. Later on, the child won't be able to describe this feeling but will have a secure feeling about his or her mother. The baby that saw an angry and frustrated look on his or her mother while feeding and felt the mother tense and unloving most of the time will feel insecure with his or her mother and maybe keep its distance as an older child. The child won't know why he or she feels this way about his/her mother but will remain mistrustful.

Worse yet, let's imagine a baby boy was picked up and shaken by its mother's boyfriend, in an angry frightening way. Let's also imagine that this man wore a beard. This baby would have an unconscious memory that being held was hurtful and frightening and might also react with fear when a man with a beard picked him up. If this baby were placed in a foster home where the foster father had a beard, it may take a very long time for the baby to trust that the foster father wouldn't hurt him. The memory of the boyfriend would be imbedded in the limbic part of the brain without the baby even knowing this.

I remember a case I had where the boy had been abused by his father and step mother. The boy was apprehended by Child Welfare and placed in a kind foster family. The boy was frightened of the foster father who was a nurturing and supportive man. If the foster father raised his arms to reach for an object or tried to hug this boy, the boy would recoil in fear. The biological father denied physically abusing his son, but we knew from the scars on the boy's body and his behaviour that he had been severely abused. The foster father was very sensitive to this boy being triggered by him and was patient and accepting of the boy's fear of him and the boy's need to remain distant.

The limbic system or emotional brain is also negatively impacted by traumatic experiences, including abuse, neglect or early loss of a caregiver. It's the part of our brain that's most sensitive to danger and will respond with protective strategies when it experiences fear and cannot turn to a protective attachment figure for safety and comfort. Infants instinctively go to their parents or caregiving person when they experience fear or danger. If this person is the source of the fear or not protective, this part of the brain will use other protective strategies like fighting back, fleeing from the danger or just freezing.

Again, I'll use Marjorie as an example. When Marjorie figured out that the nice physical touching her father was giving her was bad and not part of any loving caring behaviour, she did not want this anymore. She couldn't go to her mother for protection since her mother seemed frightened of her father. She couldn't fight back or run away since she was only three. So Marjorie learned at a very early age just to freeze and try and not feel anything when her father was touching her. She wasn't always successful in blocking the pleasure because her primitive brain was doing its job of finding physical pleasure from the touch of a parent, even an abusive one. Marjorie was a very confused and frightened three-year-old.

The largest and most advanced developed part of our brain is the **Neo-cortex** . It's the part of the brain that makes us uniquely human. It is much larger than that other parts of the brain. It's the part of our brain that allows us to think rationally, develop language, make complex decisions and use our capacity for judgement. The Neo-cortex allows us to think flexibly, to develop abstract complex thoughts and theories and to communicate ideas in words to other humans. It's the part of our brain that is able to both go inward and be aware of our feelings and body sensations and also be aware of our external world. By being aware of both external and internal stimuli and evaluating both types of information, the cortex can make rational and balanced decisions. We can also communicate in words our internal emotional states because of this part of the brain.

Let me give you an example of how the Neo-cortex functions as the integrator of what is happening outside in the world and what we are experiencing inside our bodies.

I took my car in for repair one day and arranged to have it picked up after work. The car repair person and I agreed that my key would be left under the mat of the front seat. The car would be parked behind the garage.

I left work later than I planned so it was quite dark when I walked toward the parking area of the garage. I was thinking about a case when I experienced a tightness in my stomach. I looked about and realized I was walking down a dark laneway. I realized that the tightness in my stomach was my anxiety being alone in an isolated laneway. I was carrying my briefcase and reassured myself if anyone attacked me I would hit them with my briefcase. This was a crazy thought but somehow it reassured me that I had some protection.

I saw my car, felt relief, and felt my stomach relax as I hurried toward it. I felt my stomach tense up again and then thoughts formed that someone could be in my car. It had been left unlocked. I reassured myself again that I would first look in my car before entering it. I did this, and seeing no one, opened the door, quickly went into the car and locked the door. Only then did I feel somewhat safe and found the key. I was obviously still feeling anxious because I immediately started the car and made a bee line out of the dark parking area.

If we could be observing my brain during this process we would see the neurotransmitters, rapidly moving from my stomach to my Limbic System where I experienced the anxiety, to my sight area where I could look at my environment to see what was causing this, to my Neo-cortex where my rational thinking judged that I was safe and could protect myself. The neurons travelled back to my Limbic System where the anxiety was reduced and therefore the tension in my stomach eased. The Neo-cortex or Rational Brain was able to go inward to access my body sensation, recognize anxious feelings, go outward to look at the environment and determine what was causing the anxiety. The Neo-cortex determined that there was no serious danger in the environment and sent this message to my Limbic System which reduced the anxiety. This process happened a couple of times.

For people whose brain structure and chemistry haven't developed to their best potential, the Neo-cortex can't function in this integrative and rational manner. For people who suffered trauma, the body's reaction is so intense that the rational brain cannot do its job. Or the rational brain has distorted perceptions and will see danger where none exists.

The neo-cortex is also the part of the brain that allows us to bring into conscious awareness the unconscious attachment patterns that influence our perception of ourselves and our expectations of relationships. These unconscious memories, perceptions and beliefs are stored in the limbic system. When we use our rational brain, the neo-cortex, we think about what we are feeling, how we are reacting to events and what our beliefs are. We can understand and change those feelings, reactions and beliefs that aren't helpful or not relevant to our present lives and experiences. This is the part that we'll be working on as we discuss how to change in Chapter 7.

Why should you have an understanding of your brain?

If you're a person who has difficulty controlling your impulses and your emotions, it's important for you to realize that you're not a bad person who deliberately wants to hurt other people or make relationships difficult. You may have experienced enough instability in your early relationships with your parents or caregivers that your brain chemistry was compromised and it is genuinely difficult for you to control your emotions and certainly to calm your emotions once feelings such as anger, anxiety and fear are activated.

If you're a person who is overly controlled emotionally or doesn't feel much at all, you also may have learned early on that there was no point in expressing your feelings and needs or it was dangerous to do so. Your brain chemistry shut down at an early age and your memory of how and why this happened are buried deep in your Limbic System. The links or transmitters from your Limbic System to your Neo-cortex may be limited so you make decisions that are based on rationality only, rather than the integration of both your internal emotional state and the external world.

Both being too emotional and not emotional cause problems in close relationships.

If you were raised in an environment in which you were abused, physically, emotionally and/or sexually or in which you experienced severe neglect, your Limbic System used its protective strategies to protect you and signalled your Brainstem to act with protective behaviour. Your adult brain will continue to be highly alert to danger in the environment and may distort your perception of situations and people. You may see or feel danger when none exists, or you may believe someone is threatening to you when they are not.

Remember that the brain responds to danger by using fight, flight or freeze strategies, any or all of these. So, some people will become aggressive if they think someone is dangerous. Other people will do anything to avoid conflict or avoid someone who appears unsafe to them. And other people won't feel anything and not be able to move if they sense danger. All of these are strategies the brain develops probably based on one's personality at an early age and what the brain figures is the best way to protect oneself. If the person hurting you is bigger and more powerful, the brain figures out there's no point in fighting back. That child will learn to avoid the abusive person if possible. If this becomes impossible the brain will tell the body to freeze, not feel anything and not react. This would probably keep the child safer than if he or she reacted.

People who experienced trauma as children often are limited in their ability to figure out what is reality and what is not. They may respond to body sensations or something they see or hear or feel inside with inappropriate responses. Such a person may become aggressive when someone just bumps him accidently or may withdraw when he or she hears angry voices. Both responses are based on frightening experiences from childhood that are no longer accurate in the present.

Let's pretend that we are inside the brain of Gregory, the young man who was adopted at four years of age. Little was known about his biological parents or when and why he was placed in an orphanage. It was shortly after his birth. Gregory spent the first four years of his life in the orphanage which had limited resources and a poor caretaker/child ratio. This meant that Gregory received minimal and inconsistent caregiving in his infancy. His Brain Stem or Primitive Brain probably remained in a state of anxiety and fear as an infant since his basic needs were not met. His brain chemistry wasn't in balance at an early age, with the chemical for fear and anxiety, called Cortisol, overdeveloped and the chemicals that stabilize emotions and bring peaceful feelings less developed. This is a simplistic understanding of brain chemistry but helps clarify Gregory's unregulated emotional states.

Gregory also learned that the best strategy for getting basic needs met in the orphanage, whether food or toys, was aggression. He learned to grab food from other children and be the first to have whatever toys were available. He didn't trust that the adults would take care of him, protect him or love him. His belief, internalized in his Limbic System, by a very early age, was to take care of himself, control his environment to ensure his safety and not trust adult caregivers. He remained vigilant about his environment, always ready either to be aggressive to protect himself or to run away.

Because the Brain Stem and Limbic system were not developed to their full potential in Gregory's brain, the advanced part of his brain, the Neo-cortex, was not able to function to its optimal potential. Gregory had difficulty in his language development, in his ability to learn in school, to use abstract thinking and to use good judgement in his decisions.

After being adopted Gregory's life continued to be difficult. His adoptive mother died a year after his adoption and his father, because of his own Adult Attachment Type, was incapable of being emotionally available. Gregory's belief and expectations, embedded in his Limbic System, that no one would be available and protective, were confirmed by these other life experiences. This belief and these expectations became his template for relationships. He carried this belief into the school, where he became defiant of the teachers, had difficulty with his peers and refused to do his academic work. His teachers and peers were rejecting and punitive, thus further confirming for Gregory that the world wasn't to be trusted.

Therapy impacted on these beliefs and Gregory is more capable of stable emotional and social relationships. Yet, these beliefs about not trusting others and the belief that Gregory isn't lovable remain some of his views and expectations as a young man. Gregory's brain chemistry is more balanced as a young adult and he is more able to control his aggressive tendencies. Because of his fear that he may overreact and get in trouble and his mistrust of others, he lives a more reclusive life style. He continues to have a few close friends because he has learned that having friends is fun and comforting at times.

Another example is Marjorie, the woman who had been abused as a child. An incident that Marjorie described and that I mentioned in Chapter 3 helped me realize that Marjorie had retained a memory of her father's voice in her Limbic System which impacted on her life as an adult. She continued to react to loud voices by her protective strategy of withdrawing and freezing. A supervisor at her place of employment raised her voice in a comment to Marjorie, in front of other colleagues. I don't know how loud the supervisor's voice was but to Marjorie it was threatening and debilitating. I was able to help her understand that her supervisor's voice had activated the memory of her father's voice deeply stored in her brain. She felt the same terror that her father had made her feel although this supervisor was not abusive and could not hurt Marjorie.

These two examples are of children who experienced severe neglect and abuse. Most of us have not had such extreme childhood experiences. But many of us have had childhood experiences where we had parents or caregivers who were inconsistently available or unavailable and rejecting. These patterns of interaction are also imbedded in our brains and continue to operate outside of our conscious awareness. Such patterns developed and are internalized in you because they occurred hundreds and thousands of times in your interaction with your parents or caregivers. You may not remember such interactions when you were an infant and certainly not be able to describe them. They're stored as Implicit Memories or emotional memories in the Limbic System.

What are **Implicit Memories**? The brain is capable of taking in non-verbal memories when we are infants. We develop verbal or Explicit Memories when we have the capacity for some language development. This usually occurs about 2 years of age and older. Implicit Memories are those memories based on our senses, our feelings and our automatic instinctive responses. Implicit Memories, although not conscious, do create perceptions, expectations and models for relationships. For instance, a positive implicit memory would be one where a baby comes to recognize the smell of its mother and associates this smell with the mother breast feeding and relieving the hunger sensation. This baby may always associate the smell of its mother which may be her natural body smell, her creams or her perfume with a good feeling.

Let me give you an example from my past. For years as a child and young adult I had a pleasurable feeling to a certain scent of face powder. I had this inkling of a distant memory but could never make the association. One day when I briefly whiffed this scent on a passing stranger, I had a clear vision of this face powder sitting on the dresser in my parents' bedroom. I don't have any clarity why this scent is associated with pleasure but assume it is connected to my mother's expression of love for me. Unfortunately, this scent has long been discontinued so it will not bring back that memory. I cannot retrieve any other conscious memories associated with the scent.

Another more negative implicit memory may be the smell of beer or other alcohol. I had a client whose father would become violent and beat his children after he had been drinking. She and her siblings knew if they smelled beer on their father's breath they were to hide in their bedroom and try to avoid their father. My client was a baby when she made this association, probably sensing the fear in her mother and siblings that the father was dangerous. The problems with such an implicit memory is that it continues to influence a person's reactions in his or present life. My client for years couldn't understand why the smell of beer made her so anxious with the intense desire to run away.

Implicit Memories create expectations that can be positive or negative. These are encoded or printed on our brains. They're also necessary for some of our automatic learning. We encode memories such as riding a bike, driving a car, playing an instrument and many other activities after doing such activities many times. We no longer have to think about the step by step process of such activities. They're stored in our brains and we do them naturally and without conscious awareness.

These are different from the memory you can recall when you were an older child and fell off your bike or hurt yourself in some way. Such memories are called **Explicit Memories** because you can describe in words the experience of what happened to you at that time. Such memories develop when a child has enough language development to store the events that happened with pictures associated with words. Most of the early memories that we can retrieve and describe happen at two years of age and older. Marjorie, the woman who was abused, knows the abuse started at least when she was three. She had an explicit memory that she could describe of her father touching her and then putting her in the closet when her mother called out for her.

Having this explicit memory was very helpful to Marjorie in her recognition that the abuse started at a very young age when she wouldn't have understood its meaning. This awareness helped in Marjorie's resolution that she was a young and innocent victim of her father's abuse and not capable of reciprocating.

Even the tasks I described like riding a bike can be made into Explicit Memories. If I asked, most of you can describe how you get on the bike, how you get the pedals moving, how you balance the bike and how you use the brakes to stop. The brain holds such functional memories as Implicit Memories for efficiency and ease of living. Can you imagine how difficult our daily lives would be if we had to remember in detail how to start a car, put it in the proper gear, push the accelerator, turn the wheel, etc? And I am describing a car with automatic gear shift.

Our Attachment Patterns usually operate at the level of implicit memory. You would not have awareness or memory of your mother's breast-feeding, both easing your hunger drive and creating a sense of safety and warmth. Nor would you have the memory of no mother available and crying and crying in hunger until you shut down and repressed that hungry feeling. Yet you may be aware of looking forward to meals and enjoying that time both for the good food and the interactions with family or friends. Or you may be aware of needing to ensure there's always food around and eating your meals fast. You may be aware of anxious feelings associated with the feeling of hunger. Or you may not even feel hunger just know you need to eat three meals a day. If I asked you, you may not be able to explain why you need to have food nearby or why you don't feel hunger.

We don't have a memory of our mother laughing as she changed the diaper and we peed or pooed again on the clean diaper. We don't have a memory of our mother becoming angry and yelling from the same experience. Yet I know of adoptive children who are terrified when they wet the bed and try and hide the sheets. This reaction isn't based on the reaction of the adoptive parent who is kind and understanding assuring the child that no punishment will happen. It's based on their early experiences although this may not be documented and they can't remember this past punishment.

I worked with a young girl who came from a poor orphanage. She was adopted at 18 months to a lovely family who were reasonably affluent. By three years of age she was obsessed with food. She would sneak food from cupboards that she could reach, steal candies from her brothers and hide food in her room. By the time she entered kindergarten her need for food had intensified. She would eat her whole lunch on the bus, steal food from the lunches of the other children, tell her teacher that her mother didn't give her lunch and generally find food wherever she could. Her adoptive mother was frustrated and felt helpless to stop this behaviour.

In her therapy I reflected in simple language that I wondered if she had felt hungry in the baby home in Europe and felt that no one would feed her. She cried and cried, finding some comfort in her mother's arms. It was very difficult for this child to gain a secure feeling that food would be available and although she improved in her anxiety regarding food she remains vulnerable to this day. The need for food operates in the most primitive part of the brain so children who were so deprived as infants have a difficult time changing the primitive fear of starvation.

Attachment patterns operate at the level of implicit memory because the child's need for the Attachment Figure occurs very early in development. The child usually has a primary attachment figure who responds in a patterned way to the child's needs, wants and feelings. The adult and child create a pattern similar to a dance between two people learning to respond to each other. This dance consists of the expression of needs by the infant and the response by the caregiver. Over time the child learns the dance movements of the caregiver from the many repetitive movements that occur. The caregiver unknowingly teaches the infant\child how to follow him or her even if the teaching isn't helpful to the child. The dance may allow the child to feel pleasure, joy, and safety or to feel pain, unpredictability and danger.

The child continues to practice this dance with others into adolescence and adulthood. Like many of the dances we learn, the movements are automatic, stored in implicit memory. Perhaps the adolescent or adult may have noticed that other people dance better with more flow and ease with each other. Perhaps the adult learns there are proper steps and movements to dances. Perhaps the adult meets someone who's a wonderful dancer and wants to dance with that adult. Although interested and attracted to the wonderful dancer, the adult is too frightened to risk trying the new dance. It feels safer to continue the old patterns, even knowing there are better and more pleasurable ones. But maybe the adult wants to change his/her more primitive dance patterns and learn the correct way to dance.

Changing old dance patterns isn't easy. To change such patterns, we have to come to understand our automatic expectations and movements. To learn a new dance, you have to examine the steps and method you were taught, recognize these were not correct or at least not the best way to perform the dance and relearn other steps and movements. You have to think about what you're doing, watch and learn how better to do the dance, practice, feel frustrated, lost and inadequate and eventually master the new way of doing the dance.

Undoing or deconstructing your attachment patterns and constructing new ones is similar. You'll have to learn what happened to you as a child, how you innocently came to learn how to relate to other people to have your needs, wants and feelings met, examine these patterns in some detail, stop repeating them, learn there are more effective and healthier ways to be in relationships, practice these new ways, feel frustrated, lost and inadequate and eventually master the new Attachment patterns.

Chapter 6

ADULT ATTACHMENT
AND CHOOSING A PARTNER

For adults, relationships have a fundamental paradox. We are born to be in relationships and to be close to a caregiver to have our basic needs for love, care, safety and support met. This basic drive continues into adulthood but by adulthood our early and later childhood experiences guide the choice of our partner in adult relationships. The choice of a partner may deprive us of many of our basic needs, but we tend to remain in these relationships from the primitive need to be close to someone.

By adulthood our Attachment Styles are deeply embedded in our personalities, impacted by our early childhood and later life experiences. Most people have little awareness of the impact of their childhood or even believe it was positive when there is little evidence of this. Other people believe their early childhood experiences are not influencing their adult personalities and the choices made as adults. The tragedy of such lack of awareness is that these imbedded ways of being in relationships very much influence choices of partners and behaviours in the relationship with such partners. Here are some examples that may sound familiar to your situation or someone you know.

Joanne was a creative and emotional person. She was a little overweight and never considered herself to be particularly pretty. She met Ryan at a party and noticed him immediately. He was very handsome and fit. To her surprise he approached her and they began to talk. He told her about his business and she talked about her work as an interior decorator. He asked for her phone number and she gave it to him. She never believed he would call. She perceived him as perfect and never imagined that he would want her. Ryan not only called but pursued Joanne. She was somewhat reticent to get involved since she felt inferior to Ryan and believed he would dump her once he got to know her.

She was attracted to Ryan because he appeared stable, successful, disciplined and was certainly very attractive. She thought he would be good for her since she was more emotional, self-doubting and dependent and often felt anxious and angry. She did worry sometimes when he was away for business trips but he always called her and told her that he missed her. She rarely demonstrated or expressed her insecure feelings to Ryan.

He would plan the activities on their dates and encouraged her to be more active and fit. He did this in a way that felt caring and supportive of her. She began to be more active and engaged in all the physical activities that Ryan organized for them. She grew dependent on him to do this. He wanted to be in control and his control made her feel secure. She continued to feel inferior to him and insecure but Ryan clearly wanted her, eventually asking her to marry him. She agreed to marry this perfect man.

Once they were married and living together Joanne began to feel that Ryan was less available. He worked very hard, went to the gym after work and came home tired and hungry, making his own meals. Joanne had a more regular job. She was home earlier than Ryan, too tired to work out at any gym and found herself waiting for Ryan, not sure if she should cook for him or not. She began to think his work and fitness were more important than her. She began to wonder if there was someone else he was involved with and she started to feel very anxious and angry. She didn't express these feelings to Ryan until one evening he came home particularly late and commented on how she needed to get more disciplined about losing weight and working out. Joanne lost it. She began yelling at Ryan that he was never at home, didn't seem to love her anymore and that she hated him. After screaming at him, she broke down and cried. Ryan took her in his arms, reassured her that he loved her, that he had to work late at times so he could make a good living for them. His reassurances calmed her and she apologized for her outburst. They had a good evening after this episode with both promising to change.

However, this pattern became part of their everyday life and certainly part of Joanne's internal world. She would ruminate about Ryan with growing anger and resentment. She tried to tell Ryan that she felt so abandoned and devalued by him. She couldn't contain her anger and would have frequent bouts of rage, followed by crying and isolating herself. She could feel his growing frustration with her and his withdrawal from the relationship. Finally, he told her that she was crazy and threatened to leave if she didn't change.

So how did these people come together and what factors drove them apart. Joanne has a Preoccupied/Anxious form of Adult Attachment. Consciously she chose Ryan as her boyfriend and then husband believing he was strong, stable, active, an initiator and successful. She believed, again consciously, that he would be good for her in that he encouraged her to be more fit, he organized their social and personal life and he seemed to value her creative and emotional qualities. At an unconscious level Joanne expected intimate others to be inconsistently available, to devalue her and not to be empathic to her needs and emotions in any predictable manner. Ryan met her unconscious expectations in that he was more invested in his professional and physical performance and was afraid of true intimacy. He was critical of Joanne because she wasn't disciplined, not slim and fit, and not rational enough.

So why did Ryan choose Joanne? Ryan has a Dismissing Adult Attachment (Avoidant). He was successful at his career, was extremely slim and fit, was fiercely independent and controlling and very rational. Although he wasn't in touch with his feelings in many ways, he did have a sense of his loneliness and longing for an emotional connection. He consciously thought he found this in Joanne. She was warm, funny, creative and very likeable. He knew she was overweight and not active and fit but he believed he could change this. He organized activities for them as they were dating and she accepted these without protest, even welcoming his control of their social life. He believed her warmth, capacity for emotional closeness and creativity would bring him the fulfillment in a relationship he needed.

Unconsciously Ryan didn't expect anyone to be emotionally available and supportive of him. He had learned in his family to be very independent and to achieve success by "pulling up his own boot straps." Failure hadn't been tolerated in his family. As a child and adolescent when he did feel scared and inadequate he didn't share these feelings or seek support or solace. He would go off on his own, work out the solutions to his dilemma and do whatever action was required. He came to believe he could achieve success simply by pushing himself, not tolerating weakness and always figuring out rational solutions to any problems. He also projected this belief onto others and had little respect for anyone that wasn't driven and disciplined.

So, Joanne and Ryan ended up fulfilling each other's expectations of relationships and perception of self at this unaware level of Attachment. Ryan's greater involvement in his business and fitness confirmed for Joanne that no one was available to her on a consistent basis. Ryan's criticism of her confirmed her self-perception that she was undeserving of love and respect. Her intense emotional demands did bring her attention initially but eventually, as she expected, pushed him away. Her dependency and fear of losing him would feel so strong she would attempt to bring Ryan close again. She would apologize for her behaviour and remain calm for a short period of time. She could not sustain this because Ryan would become more distant by being busy with activities. Joanne's anger would flare up again and she couldn't contain it. Her anger would drive Ryan away.

Ryan believed unconsciously that he shouldn't trust anyone to be emotionally available to him and that he had to be independent, rational and self-sufficient to achieve success. Initially he welcomed Joanne's dependency on him because it allowed him to be in control of the relationship. He continued to put more of his attention and commitment to his work and personal fitness than to his personal relationships, as he had always done. He expected Joanne to continue to idealize him and accept the degree of intimacy he could offer. He needed to be in control of how close they would be.

Joanne's emotional outbursts in the initial phase of their relationship were puzzling and upsetting to him. However, his rational talking and soothing enabled her to gain control and confirmed for him that being rational and the problem solver was his best role. Over time Ryan began to feel more deprived and resentful. Joanne's inability to lose weight and become fit left Ryan feeling angry and disdainful of Joanne and his value for her emotional availability and creativity waned. He even began to demonstrate that he was as creative as her, demeaning her particular gift and talent. He became more distant and independent confirming for Joanne that no one was emotionally available to her and she became more emotionally uncontrollable confirming for him that no one was going to care and nurture him. They remained in this mutually unhappy and unfulfilling relationship because Joanne was so dependent and terrified of being autonomous and Ryan couldn't tolerate the feeling that he had failed in his marriage. How sad for each of them.

It isn't unusual to find this pattern in intimate relationships where emotional people mate with emotionally unavailable people. Each believes at the level of awareness that the other person will complement them and bring to the relationship what is lacking in the other. The emotionally unstable person believes the strong independent person will bring stability, security and safety. She doesn't recognize that such independence is based on a weak foundation that includes mistrust and the repression of needs and emotions. The emotionally stifled person believes the emotionally expressive person will offer him/her the love, nurturing and warmth that was missing in his/her childhood He/she doesn't recognize that such intense expression of emotions is based on deep insecurity and a fear and oversensitivity that he won't be consistently available. Once intimacy is established each discovers that their conscious hopes and wishes aren't fulfilled and their early childhood experiences are repeated.

How do we understand men and women who chose abusive partners and remain in these abusive relationships. They tolerate physical and emotional abuse justifying this by a number of rationalizations. They may state that their husbands/partners are abusive only when they're drunk. They're remorseful and apologetic after their drunken abusive behaviour, even remaining loving and complimentary until the next bout of drinking. These women/men may blame themselves for the abuse, finding fault in their own housekeeping, parenting, attractiveness, or nagging personality. Even when they leave their partners because families, social services or the law intervenes they will return and repeat their patterns.

This tolerance for abuse may be puzzling to many people but Attachment Theory helps us understand the unaware motivation and dynamics. Most of these women/men have suffered abuse in their childhood.

Therefore, their belief about themselves is that they are unworthy of love and kindness and respect and their expectations of relationships is that they will be abused and treated badly. When they are treated this way by their boyfriends/girlfriends and spouses the treatment confirms for them the deeply held self-image they are unworthy and repeats what is familiar from childhood—abuse and neglect.

Even when such abusive relationships terminate either because the woman/man finds the strength to do this, or her/his partner leaves or is arrested and forced to leave, such women/men are likely to enter into another abusive relationship. Without becoming aware of the unconscious drive to develop harmful relationships such women/men are doomed to repeat them.

We also need to understand the people who are the abusers. Such men/women have also come from dangerous and traumatic families or institutional environments. They may have learned to protect themselves by being aggressive and controlling. Their view of the world is that it is dangerous, people cannot be trusted and one must be vigilant, in control and aggressive to be self-protective. Such men/women can easily distort innocent behaviours as belligerent and harmful to them. When they're drinking their perception of people and situations is more distorted and their self-control is more inhibited. They may experience a wife/partner who isn't at home as threatening; they may experience any move of independence by a wife/partner as dangerous; and they may experience their wife's involvement with a friend or family member as undermining their power and control. Their only strategy to regain control and safety is to become aggressive. When this is successful, since such wives/partners acquiesce to the violence, they feel safe.

I'm not in any manner justifying violence or abuse. I'm explaining from the lens of Attachment Theory how such people developed their abusive pattern in relationships. Such abusers can be taught to control their rage and learn strategies to modify their behaviour. However, unless they also understand the underlying and unconscious beliefs and perceptions they hold of themselves, others, social situations and the world, they're likely to repeat such patterns in close relationships and social situations.

How do we explain someone like Marjorie who, in spite of her early severe abuse, chose a husband who was protective and nurturing? Fortunately for Marjorie she found a priest in her teenage years that she confided in about the abuse. The priest informed Marjorie that her father was wholly responsible for the abuse and that Marjorie was an innocent victim. This person was someone Marjorie respected and he offered to come to her home and confront her father. Marjorie didn't allow this but his reflections empowered Marjorie and she was able to confront her father and stop the abuse.

This reality feedback also enabled Marjorie to perceive her father as disgusting and evil and to consciously choose someone who was physically different than her father. Fortunately for Marjorie her physical choice of a husband also included a caring and protective man who was attracted to her innocence and naivety. Perhaps he was too protective but this was a far better quality for Marjorie than someone who was abusive. So, both Marjorie's conscious choice and luck or good fortune combined to assist her in choosing a partner who did not confirm for her she was only deserving of abuse. Her choice however didn't enable her to share her inner world of self-hate and fear and she didn't resolve her early childhood trauma until much later in her life. So, for Marjorie there was protection but not enough encouragement to confront her fears, in her choice of husband.

It's not unusual for many of us to tell ourselves we won't choose someone like our mothers or fathers or to tell ourselves we won't be like our mothers or fathers. This is particularly true for people who have witnessed abuse in their childhood homes but also true for children who have witnessed conflict between parents and who are aware of one or both parents being unhappy. To decide at a conscious level that you won't marry an alcoholic or angry abusive man or woman is a healthy decision. Such decisions may help you avoid someone who clearly drinks too much or is unable to manage his or her anger. For a child to see his or her mother unhappy and complaining that his or her father is always working and never home for them may influence that child to find a spouse who isn't a workaholic and is more available for the family. Conscious choices based on both positive and negative childhood experiences can be helpful in adult choices of partners or spouses.

But the unconscious is always lurking and pointing us in directions that surprise us. This is why we're so astonished when we find ourselves married or partnered to that person we were determined not to select.

I have a distinct memory of observing my mother very distraught by some conflict she had with my father. She was in my parents' bedroom crying intensely, barely able to talk, tears streaming down her face and looking terrible and so vulnerable. I had never seen my mother so emotionally upset and didn't like what I saw. I also idealized my father so couldn't accept her angry words about what he'd done to emotionally upset her. I recall consciously deciding never to be so emotionally upset and vulnerable and therefore never allowing anyone to hurt me to that extent. My mother and I never discussed then or later in my life what had happened that day and its impact on me. I didn't fully process this experience, so the incident remained in my conscious memory bank as an unwanted experience never to be replicated in my personal life.

I lived by this motto into my adult life, not only because of this one conscious experience. My mother's early childhood had been fraught with abuse and neglect by her father both against her and her siblings and more significantly by her father's severe abuse of her mother. She had consciously left her home in Europe to better her life in Canada. She arrived as a young person with the profound belief that the world was unsafe and that she had to take care of herself. No one would be available to take care of her and protect her. Her later life experiences in Canada continued to confirm this reality for her.

My mother built a fortress around herself, holding a belief that one should be fiercely independent and never trust anyone. She consciously and unconsciously transmitted this view to me. Which is why it was so astounding and confusing to me to witness my mother so distraught. I never saw her so upset again and I am sure my father's behaviour reinforced her unconscious belief not to get close to anyone and not allow anyone to hurt you.

I offer this experience as an example of both a conscious and unconscious experience that I internalized. I recall consciously an unpleasant memory of my mother being emotionally distraught because of her relationship with my father. She was clearly hurt, appearing vulnerable and unattractive. However, this incident was so profound for me because of the experiences and belief imbedded in my unconscious memory from my relationship with my mother that being emotional and vulnerable was dangerous and to be avoided. She confirmed for me that being intimate and dependent in a marriage was not safe.

We choose our partners based on both conscious and unconscious motivations. This book focuses on the unconscious or unaware forces that spur us to choose the partners we do. Most of us can describe reasons why we chose our partners and can describe our experiences in our past and present relationships. We can all answer the questions posed in questionnaires about our romantic relationships. The limitations in our answers and descriptions is that they don't address the unaware motivations for our choices which are so powerful in driving us. So, if you have been puzzled by how, in spite of your determination not to marry someone like your father or your mother, you are with such a person, you will now understand how this happened.
And how to change this pattern.

Chapter 7

CHANGING YOUR
ATTACHMENT CATEGORY

∽

B y now you probably have some idea of your Attachment Category.
If you discovered that you have an Insecure Attachment, you
may be feeling both good and discouraged. You may feel good because
you have a new way of understanding yourself that is enlightening and
exciting. You may feel discouraged because if feels almost impossible
to change the way you have been most of your life.

This chapter will focus on both understanding and changing your
Attachment Category. We discussed in Chapter 4 how to recognize your
Attachment by reviewing the descriptions of the attitudes and behaviour one demonstrates in each category. You may find that descriptions
from more than one category apply to you but most of you will find
yourselves fitting more into one category than others. This category
would be your primary Attachment pattern in relationships which
should be the focus of your attempts to change this pattern.

I will describe again the ways you behave in relationships based on a
particular Attachment Category so you can identify your own category
and then focus on the specific interventions that you'll need to apply
to change your particular Attachment Category. I will also discuss the

importance of non-judgemental awareness and accepting what you may not be able to change.

The concept of Mindfulness is well documented and discussed. Dan Siegel describes Mindfulness as "a form of mental activity that trains the mind to become aware of itself and to pay attention to one's own intention ... mindfulness requires paying attention to the present moment from a stance that is non-judgemental and nonreactive."[3] Although I won't be using this term specifically, I do believe that Mindfulness is essential to change oneself. In order to change one's Attachment Category, one must examine with self-honesty one's behaviour, emotions, beliefs, expectations and intentions in intimate relationships.

What will help you do this with at times brutal honesty is to understand that you developed your way of being in relationships innocently and out of the need for closeness and survival. You have the Attachment you have because of your childhood experiences, most likely confirmed by later life experiences. Accept this with kindness, no self-criticism and open-mindedness. This is the first step in change. You can start the process of change only from this position of being truthful to yourself and accepting this new way of understanding yourself.

Understanding yourself involves having a life story that may or may not involve painful childhood experiences but one that you have made sense of as an adult. Research on Attachment shows that "people who were securely attached tended to acknowledge both positive and negative aspects of their family experiences, and they were able to show how these experiences related to their later development. They could give a *coherent* account of their past and how they came to be who they are as adults."[4] Even people with difficult pasts can develop a

---

3 Siegel, Daniel, Mindsight, 2010, Bantam Books, New York, Pg. 86.
4 Ibid., p. 172.

believable and coherent life story allowing them to have Earned Security, by remembering, understanding and making sense of their childhood experiences.

And remember, your goal is to develop Earned Secure or Autonomous/ Secure Attachment so you experience relationships as generally safe and nurturing and you experience yourself as worthy of consistent love, caring and security. Working on yourself to develop Autonomous Attachment is a worthy goal because it will offer the following positive attributes:

- A **healthy sense of entitlement** to express your feelings, needs and wants in a relationship. A healthy sense of entitlement means that you recognize you are important enough in a relationship to let the other person understand your needs, wants and feelings but not so important that only your needs are considered or considered all the time.

- You're capable of **mutuality in intimate relationships**. This follows from the first quality that you understand that both partners in a relationship will have to experience that needs, feelings and wants are met enough of the time that there's a feeling of balance and mutuality. Security allows you to delay the fulfillment of your needs and wants at times, trusting they'll get met in the near future.

- **Acceptance of Differences**. Your partner may have a very different way of perceiving the world, different values, different behaviours in relationships and different sensibility, taste, and wants. These differences can often cause conflict because one person in the relationships thinks his or her way is right and the other wrong. Secure Autonomous people have greater capacity to see such differences as just differences without a value judgement. There may be discussion if the differences create conflict but the resolution arrives without attacks and the fight for whose way is better. Acceptance of differences allows for compromise.

- **Non-judgemental Stance**. Acceptance of differences means that you'll be less judgemental of others who are different than you. This doesn't mean that you don't have values and standards of morality and ethics. Being non-judgemental means that you are open to the reality that other people have different values, morals and ways of being and are curious about their ways, rather than quick to judge. Imagine a world where people accepted that others are different and not better or worse than one another.

- **Positive Self-regard**. People with Autonomous or Secure Attachments have both good self-worth and a realistic sense of self, accepting their imperfections and limitations.

- **Capacity for both Autonomy and Union**. People with Secure attachments have the capacity for both intimacy and independence. They value close relationships, seek them out and work at maintaining them. They also value their separateness and enjoy alone time and activities and friendships outside their primary relationship.

- **Coping with Conflict**. Secure people are able to resolve conflicts in relationships. They are more able to focus on the issue of the conflict without feeling threatened personally or without feeling their relationship is doomed. They believe in their capacity to repair the conflict although they may feel hurt and cut off during an argument.

- **Affect Regulation**. Secure people have the capacity to feel and express their emotions without being out of control. This is an important quality or strength since being able to regulate or modify your emotions is essential for not only healthy intimate relationships but for success generally in one's life.

- **Duration and Commitment**. People with Secure/Autonomous Attachments have the capacity to make long term commitments in relationships and honour such commitments. This is due to many of the attributes we mentioned above and also because there is both a general satisfaction in close relationships and reliance on such relationships for emotional support and security.

Generally, I would recommend that you see a therapist if you're having problems in your relationships and recognize that at least part of the problem is your contribution. From my perspective it would be advisable to find a therapist who has an understanding of Attachment Theory and works from this model of therapy. However, Attachment Focused Therapists are difficult to find so engaging in therapy with a good therapist that you feel comfortable with and grow to trust is a fine substitute. To make deep changes which Attachment Focused Therapy would promote, you may have to be in long term therapy. If you and your spouse/partner decide to go together you'll still need to look at your childhood history and how it is influencing your relationship in the present.

For a number of reasons, people cannot or do not want to go into therapy. So, I'll present some strategies that may be helpful in not only understanding your Attachment but also trying to change the negative ways your Attachment influences your behaviour in relationships. However, these suggestions for change are not a substitute for engaging in therapy.

Changing Your Preoccupied/Anxious Attachment

If you have determined that your Attachment Style is Preoccupied/anxious then you're likely to have the following issues in your relationships:

- You tend to be very emotional, with poor ability to regulate your emotions.
- You tend to feel anxious and angry in your close relationship.
- You are not likely to trust that your spouse or partner truly loves you and will be available to you on a consistent basis.
- You will tend to devalue yourself, feel insecure about yourself and perhaps overvalue your spouse or partner, at least in the beginning of the relationship.

- You feel most complete when you are in a relationship and become extremely dependent on an intimate other for your sense of self.
- This dependency may lead to your feeling jealous, threatened by other people or activities in the life of your partner and generally anxious and preoccupied about your spouse/partner.
- Such intense feelings can become destructive in your relationship but controlling them feels impossible for you.

These are the changes that you will have to work on, as challenging as they may be:

- Understanding your early childhood history
- Connecting this understanding to your present relationship(s)
- Mourning for what you deserved but didn't receive as a child
- Becoming more autonomous or independent
- Learning to regulate your emotions
- Expressing what you need and want more honestly, without drama and manipulation
- Developing better self-worth
- Stop blaming others for your feelings and problems
- Risk doing things differently

Your Childhood

The first step for anyone who wants to change his/her Adult Attachment is to understand how you came to be the way you are. For people with Preoccupied Anxious Attachments this usually means you had a mother or primary attachment person who wasn't consistently available. You learned that you had to express your needs and wants loudly and dramatically to be heard or had to manipulate in other ways to ensure your mother would pay attention to you. You were always watchful to make sure you didn't miss a time when your mother or caregiver was available. This meant that you became both very dependent on her and also never trusted her availability. It was hard for you to leave her and you would think about her much of the time when you were separated from her.

What you do need to understand is that this early relationship left you with a distorted view of all relationships. You continue to feel insecure, fear that no one will be available, are highly sensitive to your partner/spouse abandoning you and probably misinterpret certain behaviours and other relationships your partner/spouse may have. You did what you had to do as a young child to keep your mother/caregiver close and ensure she was available. You don't have to continue to do this in your present relationships, particularly in your intimate relationship with your spouse/partner. You have to develop other strategies to express your anxieties and needs and ensure you have a realistic view of what's happening in your relationships.

The areas and behaviours you will have to examine and change as a Preoccupied/Anxious Attached person are:

1. Regulating your emotions, particularly your anger.
2. Stopping the rumination or preoccupation about your relationships.
3. Becoming more independent and autonomous.
4. Learning to communicate your needs, wants and feelings without intense affect, drama or demanding behaviour.
5. Valuing yourself and not looking to another person to fulfill all your needs. No one can do this for you. You'll end up being angry, hurt and disappointed. You'll be puzzled how the partner you thought was so perfect is so unavailable and rejecting.

Regulating your Emotions

I explained some of the understanding of the brain in chapter 6. Your inability to control your intense feelings is related to what's happening in your brain. When you experience feelings these occur in your limbic system or your emotional brain. Because as a child you were always in a state of anxiety and anger your rational brain or Neocortex did not develop optimally. How we regulate our feelings is through the transmitters in our brain. In regulated or integrated brains the transmitters in the Limbic System relay the emotions to the Neocortex which assesses the meaning of the emotions and transmits this information back to the Limbic System and Brain Stem, so an appropriate response can be communicated. In unregulated brains the limbic system reacts without the input from the reasoning brain so a primitive emotional reaction is communicated, either with words or behaviour.

When you're feeling jealous and anxious because your husband is working late, your emotions are in high gear. Even if you know he has a legitimate business meeting that has run late, your emotions are ruling your brain. You may tell yourself that his meeting is running late but your feelings of mistrust are what drive you to call every five minutes, are why you ruminate about what he's doing, why you picture him with some woman at his office and why your anger has turned to rage. When your husband does arrive late, your limbic and brain stem is in full control and you may start screaming at your husband, maybe throw something at him and eventually cry uncontrollably. If we could look at your brain we would see the Limbic System lit up and the Neocortex fairly dormant.

You need to activate your rational brain, the Neocortex. Given the intensity and impulsivity of your emotions, you have little time to do this. Here are the steps you need to practice, over and over again.

EXERCISES

1. Know your triggers: These are related to your partner/spouse or close friend not being immediately available or not being empathic to you all the time.

2. Recognize the initial feeling of fear, anxiety and anger, in response to your triggers

3. Talk to yourself. Tell yourself you know where the feelings are coming from and are not based on reality.

4. Comfort yourself. Self-comfort has different behaviours for each person so learn what works for you when you're in such an agitated state. This can be taking a bath, going out with a friend, buying yourself a small and inexpensive item, such as a lipstick, watching your favourite TV show or even having a good cry. Try and avoid comforting yourself with eating excessively, buying expensive items, gambling, drinking or doing drugs or taking vengeance on your partner/spouse.

5. Learning to control your intense feelings by known helpful methods:

   • Deep breathing: Learn deep breathing exercises and focus on your breathing. This isn't easy for you since your preoccupied thoughts and anger will interrupt your focus on your breathing. Continue to try and refocus on your breathing every time you're distracted by your feelings of anxiety and anger.

   • Focus on other thoughts and places that are more positive or distracting. Such images can be positive times with your partner, or a positive time you had on your own somewhere, or can be thoughts about a TV program, movie you saw, book you read, concert you attended. The goal of your refocus is to break the cycle of rumination and its accompanying intense feelings.

   • Exercise: Yoga and Pilates are known exercises to help you focus on the moment but any exercise that helps you focus on your body and improving your fitness will be useful. It's better if you're playing team sports or in a group fitness program since you're forced to interact with others. However, if you're engaged in a more solitary exercise, such as jogging or walking, listen to music or a radio station.

- Talking to a friend or relative. If you know that talking to someone about your experiences and emotions does help you calm down and get a more realistic perspective on your situation then do this. Chose a person who can offer you a perspective that is reassuring and does not validate your unrealistic perception. Do not talk to someone who'll support the escalation of your feelings.

- Talking to your partner/spouse. If you know that talking to your partner or spouse will be helpful and reassuring with one phone call or email then do this. If you know that you'll need constant reassurance involving many phone calls and long periods on the phone, then don't reach out. Such intense and time consuming discussions will only alienate your partner and aggravate you. Not helpful.

- Medication. I know that this may be difficult for you to consider but it could be necessary. Preoccupied people often have a chemical imbalance because of their early upbringing. A complete explanation of your brain chemistry is complex but I'll offer a simpler understanding. Preoccupied people have an overabundance of the chemicals that arouse anxiety and anger and an undersupply of the chemicals that create a calm and contented state. Therefore they may need to take medication that boosts the brain's capacity to bring its agitated state to one of greater peacefulness.

You will need to consult with your family doctor or a psychiatrist about going on medication. Only a physician can prescribe medication.

Mourning

Preoccupied people are often still angry at their parents and may continue to be dependent on them, still hoping for the consistent love and attention. If this resonates with you, you need to accept that it is very unlikely that your relationship with your biological, adoptive or foster parents or other caregivers will change. You'll have to mourn the loss of what you longed for and didn't receive as a child and aren't receiving as an adult. All people with insecure attachments need to do this but your mourning may involve more intense feelings. You will likely need someone to help you through this process but some of the mourning will require being alone and allowing yourself to feel pain, sadness and anger. Although what you're grieving is somewhat abstract and inside you, the process is similar to that of having lost someone close to you.

The grieving process involves:

- Protest and anger: You will need to feel anger at your parent for not being available to you to meet your childhood needs and understand your feelings. You may feel the need to deny and protest that they cannot change, if they are alive. If they are deceased you may feel anger that they have left you before you could resolve your issues of attachment with them. You will need to let go of this anger in time so you can feel the pain of your loss.
- Sadness and Despair: You will need to feel a deep sense of sadness that as a very young child you were not offered the consistent love and caring you needed, which resulted in you feeling so insecure. You may need to cry and just feel the pain of your loss. If your parents are still alive you may need to take a break from your relationship with them. If you think your parents could examine their parenting of you and are open to your new understanding of their inconsistency and own preoccupation you could talk to them. During this period it would be helpful

to share your pain and sadness with your spouse/partner and seek support from him or her. Your spouse/partner may be able to offer you this help and guidance since the anger is not directed at him or her.

- Detachment: Eventually you will have to reach a feeling of healthy detachment. Such detachment will allow you to be more accepting of your parents and their limitations. It will enable you to accept what your parents can and cannot offer you in a close relationship. You will be less invested in your need for them. Your mother may still be inconsistent in her support of you as an adult but if you are no longer seeking or longing for this, you will not experience the previous anger and anxiety.

- Redeveloping your sense of self: Once you have reached a feeling of resolution and can see your parents realistically and non-judgemental- ly, you will feel a new sense of freedom and peace internally. Hopefully you will be able to be realistic and accepting of your needs and wants in your relationship and communicate these without the previous in- tensity and drama. Hopefully your spouse/partner will recognize your changes and be more receptive to meeting your needs and wants. Your new sense of self will help you look realistically at your relationship and decide if your spouse/partner is a good fit for you.

Becoming more independent

As we discussed in previous chapters, children with Anxious Ambivalent Attachment become very dependent and clingy. They're unable to move out into the world with security because their Attachment base was so insecure. When you have a mother who you know is sometimes avail- able and maybe loving and nurturing, you won't want to miss such a moment with her This may mean that you need to hang around your mother and certainly not leave her for long periods. So you end up clinging to your mother, doing everything to gain her attention but always feeling pretty helpless and anxious about this.

You may continue to feel this neediness in most relationships and tend to feel you always need to have someone close in your life to make you feel whole.

You'll have a great challenge changing this but becoming more autonomous and independent is a crucial goal for you. You'll need to feel whole and good about yourself even when you're not in an intimate relationship. This independent sense of self is what will enable you to choose someone with adult security or change the relationship you have now.

Becoming more independent can involve a number of actions:

- It is important that you have an activity that is solely yours. This can be a job, a career, a hobby, interests or friends. This activity needs to take you away from your relationship with your spouse/partner or parents. Initially you may spend your time thinking about what your spouse/partner/boyfriend/girlfriend is doing but it is important that you not contact them and focus on your independent activity. In time your activity will bring you pleasure and if it involves skill and knowledge building, it will enhance your self-worth.

- Reassuring yourself that you can manage without your partner/spouse and parents. When you feel that sense of anxiety and neediness you will have to stop yourself from calling your partner and certainly from calling him or her many times. You will have to try and complete whatever task or problem you were encountering and tell yourself you will be fine on your own. You may have to reassure yourself many many times. Again in time you will come to trust that you can manage on your own and feel the power and confidence that comes with this feeling.

Communicating your Needs,
Wants and Feelings More effectively

You learned as a young child that the way to get attention when your mother/caregiver was unavailable was to intensify your demands. Even as a baby you may have learned that if you cried louder and insistently, eventually your mother heard your cries and attended to you. The problem for you now is that you still believe you need to do these insistent and demanding calls for attention. Demanding attention as an adult usually alienates the people from whom you're seeking it.

You need to communicate your needs and wants from your spouse/partner in a way that they can hear and understand. You need to explain with feelings but not uncontrolled anger, how much you do need attention and how sensitive you are to anyone not being available and present for you. If you communicate to your spouse/partner your feelings of hurt and fear that you don't matter to him or her when he or she isn't present or available, your partner/spouse will be able to hear you. Hopefully they will become more present for you. Anger pushes people away, hurt brings them close.

Valuing Yourself

Most children who have a parent that wasn't available or inconsistently available believe it's because they're not lovable enough or worthy enough for this love and attention. Such children internalize this belief and may act in ways that validate it. Anxious/Ambivalent Attached children demand attention in inappropriate ways, are clingy and needy and may not be very likeable. They end up alienating other people in their lives such as teachers, other parents and certainly peers. This rejection by other adults and children reinforces their beliefs that they're not lovable and worthy of nurturing. By adulthood such people don't value themselves and continue to alienate people by their demands for attention and their difficult behaviour.

These are some of the actions you will need to do:

- You have to tell yourself that you are lovable and worthy of caring and attention. Your devaluing yourself is based on your sad experience in childhood and doesn't have to continue into your present life. Focus on all the positive traits you see in yourself and your accomplishments.
- If you need external reinforcement ask the people you care about in your life what they value about you. And listen to this feedback. Don't dismiss it by convincing yourself they don't really know you, that they're just being nice and not honest, or all the other ways you have of dismissing positive comments about you.
- Every day you will need to reaffirm positive views about yourself by focusing on the constructive things you did or said. If you've had a "bad" day and reverted to your more demanding and destructive patterns, you'll have to forgive yourself and assure yourself that tomorrow is a new day and you'll have many opportunities to make changes.

Remember it took many years to develop your insecure pattern of Attachment. It will take a long time to redevelop a more secure pattern of Attachment.

Changing Dismissing/Avoidant Attachment

If you've determined that your Attachment Category is Dismissing/ Avoidant then you're aware that you have difficulty developing intimacy, allowing yourself to be vulnerable and dependent and that you over- value independency and self-sufficiency. You'll have to examine and understand your particular style of being avoidant of closeness so you can implement the strategies for change I will present. Your challenge will be to stop all the activities and strategies you developed to protect yourself from closeness and tolerate the anxiety and fear that will be activated as you work at intimacy.

Understanding Your Childhood

Children with Avoidant Attachments had parents/caregivers who were unavailable, rejecting or self-centred. If you had a parent or caregiver who was consistently unavailable or rejecting, then you learned to re- press your needs, wants and feelings and avoid your parent/caregiver since you weren't going to receive love, caring and empathy anyway. If you had a narcissistic parent or caregiver who needed you to take care of her/his needs or to be the perfect child, you learned that you would be loved or valued if you met the needs of your parent and denied your own. You may have had to support a dependent mother, tell a parent constantly how wonderful he or she was, perform perfectly in activities and academically so your parent looked good or made sure that you looked good and behaved well as a reflection of your parent.

If you had an authoritarian parent who demanded obedience and per- fection, you learned that, if you were compliant, well-behaved and successful in school and extra-curricular activities, you received the approval of your parent. If you weren't able to perform as your parent expected and needed, you were belittled and rejected.

If you had the kind of parent described above, you learned to take care of yourself and not rely on the adults in your life to take care of you. The sad reality for such children is that they may appear independent, strong, self-assured and successful. Other adults such a teachers, coaches and other parents turn to them to be the helpers or at least rely on them to be the non-problematic children. If you were a child who performed well in school and in your other activities you would receive praise for this and continue to believe you were valued because of your performance, not for being you. Such children aren't recognized by teachers or other adults as vulnerable children who need attention and support. The reality is that Avoidant Children's appearance of independence and success is based on a weak foundation.

As an adult you may be very successful in your profession, business, job, and other activities but not in your intimate relationships. Your partner/spouse may complain about your lack of emotions, your inability to express affection, your spending more time at work than with your spouse and your general distance from him or her. Depending on your awareness and how in touch with feelings you are, you may understand how difficult your distancing is for your spouse. Or you may truly not understand what your spouse is needing since you provide a stable and rich life style for your spouse. You provide all the material things he/she needs and still he/she is unhappy.

The areas you will need to examine and change are:
1. Your limitation or inability to allow yourself to feel.
2. Your fear of being dependent on others and experiencing vulnerability.
3. Your difficulty expressing what you need, want and feel when you are in touch with such inner states.
4. Your strategies for avoiding intimacy, such as being constantly busy, being a workaholic, being a caregiver, needing to socialize much of the time or being isolated much of the time or never making a commitment to a relationship.

5. Your need to control your relationships or your environment

6. Being sexually promiscuous, valuing the sexual relationship but not wanting emotional closeness or not engaging in sex in close relationships.

7. Valuing intellect over emotions

8. Viewing yourself as superior to others

Let's look at how you can begin to change these areas.

1. Allowing Yourself to Feel

You'll have to ask yourself regularly how you're feeling about your relationship or problems that occur in them. You'll have to work at stopping your logical brain from giving you and your partner/spouse the answers. Go inward and take the time to get in touch with what you're feeling. This can be anger, sadness, anxiety or fear. You can even pause to feel pleasure and happiness. Stay with the feelings before thinking about what is activating such feelings and how to solve these issues. You can try some activities that may help with becoming aware of feelings:

Drawing: Allow yourself to draw and colour whatever comes to mind. Don't worry about drawing well or accurately. Add colour to your drawing. When it's finished ask yourself what feelings are evoked by the drawing. You may want to ask someone you trust, even a little, their impressions of your drawing. Write them down. Reflect on the feelings. Don't analyze the drawing.

Looking at pictures that show faces: Look at magazines, find faces, ask yourself what feelings the different facial expressions evoke for you.

Look at pictures from your past: See if you can tell what you may have been feeling as a child, adolescent or young adult from pictures or videos you may have. Allow yourself to feel sorry for the younger you who had to be so perfect, so closed down, such a caretaker of others and so independent and alone.

2. Becoming More Dependent and Vulnerable

This will be a great challenge for you. You truly believe that you can't trust anyone to understand your inner world and be available to offer support, validation or a hug and kiss. And yet becoming more dependent is essential for you to gain the wonderful feeling that someone is really in your corner to promote and encourage you for your own needs and wants, not for theirs.

So you'll need to reach out when you feel the doubt about your performance at work, or in other activities or just about yourself. You'll need to tell your spouse/partner how you're feeling and ask for her/his support. Remember your spouse by now has learned that you fix your own problems so may be surprised by your reaching out to her or him. You'll need to engage with your spouse in this emotional dialogue although all your inner voices are pushing you to devalue this relationship and go back to being alone and independent. Don't listen to those old voices. You're striving for a new balanced you who can rely on others.

You will have to find ways to control or modify your anxiety as your fear of closeness emerges. Similar to the previous section you will need to:

- Use breathing exercises
- Leave the situation if it is too overwhelming. Tell your spouse/partner you are doing this because opening up to her/him is so anxiety provoking. Leave, lower your anxiety and then return to continue the dialogue.
- Think about places, situations or people that can ground you to a more peaceful state.
- Try and have your spouse comfort you by just holding your hand, giving you a hug or just sitting quietly with you. You do not have to talk about anything during this comforting time.
- If you become overwhelmed with anxiety as you reach for closeness, take a break from the process. Allow yourself your old defenses such as working, playing a sport or being on your computer for a lengthy time. This avoidance pattern should be for a brief period, even one day, to reduce the level of anxiety. You will have to reassure yourself, that you will be emotionally stable again and will continue the process of learning to be intimate.

3. Determining Your Own Needs and Wants

You'll need to spend some time with yourself, giving yourself permission to explore what it is you need and want in your relationships. If this is difficult, allow yourself to fantasize what the perfect relationship would look like to you and for you. Write down at least one need that you would want to have your spouse meet and one want you would like to experience. If you're able to do this, write down as well the feelings you have about not having this need and want met by your spouse. Such feelings can be anger at your spouse or your parents for not meeting your needs or it can be sadness that you've been so neglected. You're allowed to feel whatever you feel to the intensity that you feel it.

Keep a journal. Write down the feelings that emerge as you try to change. Write down how you dealt with such feelings. Write about the needs and wants that you begin to experience. Practice in writing what you might say to your partner or spouse to tell them about your feeling, needs and wants.

4. Creating Intimacy

Over time you're gradually going to try and give up all the strategies that you developed from childhood to avoid intimacy. Make a list of all the ways you think you do this. Some of these may include:

- being very busy
- having conversations with your spouse only about the children, the household, your work, her work, gossip or politics and intellectual pursuits, not feelings, your worries or your relationship.
- Working long hours
- Exercising excessively
- Doing many extracurricular activities
- Spending most of your time on your computer, iPad or iPhone, even during dinner, time with your spouse or children or at bedtime.

Ask your spouse/partner the ways she sees you creating distance from her and be open to her perceptions.

Once you've itemized the ways you avoid closeness, pick one that you're prepared to work on. Pick the one that would be the easiest for you.

For example, I have a client who plays hockey many times in the week to the chagrin of his wife. She feels he spends little time with her. So, after discussing this issue, he was able to tell her that he has always wanted her to come to his games and watch him play. She has no interest in hockey but heard his invitation for closeness and agreed to go to some games. He then agreed to find something they would both enjoy.

Another client—these seem to be males but there are dismissing females —worked late every night His wife complained about this and had developed her own activities to cope with her husband's absence. He was convinced that he had to work so hard to provide for the family and also accused his wife of spending so much. I had helped him understand that he had learned as a child to be a top student in school and then university to make his parents love him and be proud of him. He continued to believe he had to be an excellent provider and the best professional in his field although this wasn't what his wife and children needed and wanted from him. He slowly began to reduce his time at the office and spend more time with his wife. Although the time spent together was focused on work around the home and cottage, his wife felt he was more available and welcomed the change.

5. Learning to be More Spontaneous

People with Dismissing Attachments tend to be more controlling since they've learned over a lifetime to control their emotions and the level of intimacy they will tolerate. They tend to have patterned life styles that don't include just spontaneously doing something for the joy and fun of it. You'll need to risk doing something spontaneous, like calling your spouse/partner suddenly and telling her/him you made a reservation at a nice restaurant or better yet a hotel room for the weekend.

6. Having Serial Sexual Relationships

If you're a single Dismissing Attached person, you may be involved in a number of relationships either serially or at one time. This is clearly a way for you to avoid intimacy but such relationships also may leave you feeling empty and alone, confirming for you your early childhood belief that no one was there to fulfill your needs. You'll need to break this pattern. You have to force yourself to stay with one person that you like, to see if the relationship can progress to one of more intimacy. You'll need to stop yourself from developing immediate sexual relationships that are superficial and emotionally unsatisfying.

If you're in a marriage or partnership and having multiple affairs you'll need to understand that such affairs allow you to avoid the issues in your marriage. You're both avoiding dealing with what is missing for you in your marriage and avoiding any future possibilities of genuine intimacy. You will need to stop the affairs and start a dialogue with your spouse/partner.

In all of these scenarios it would be wise to consult with a therapist.

7. Overvaluing Intellect

When I was a young girl, I would see and hear my older brother and father talking politics. I knew that my father was actively involved in reading about and following politics and was involved in some local politics. My mother would be in the kitchen cooking and cleaning. The expectation was that I would join her in the kitchen to help. I wanted to be and insisted that I be, in the room where my father and brother were. I became interested in politics and followed my father's leftist views of politics so I could be a part of the intellectual dyad of my brother and father. I'm not sure I ever was a validated member of that elite dyad but I sure tried to become more of an intellectual. I put aside my romance novels, my beauty magazines, or at least hid them from my brother's view and began to read more politically oriented writings. Eventually I took courses in politics and philosophy at the University. I repressed my simpler interests and creative traits to be the person my father valued.

It wasn't until my adult years I was able to understand that politics for my father was his means for fulfilling the deprivation from his childhood and for giving meaning to his life. He found it very difficult to find intimacy in just being with someone so his relationships revolved around his political beliefs and activities. When I understood his Dismissing Attachment I understood that I also had come to overvalue intellect and base my relationships on the intelligence of the other person. Fortunately for me I became a therapist, developed self-awareness and the desire to change.

Many Dismissing Attachment people use intellectualization and being rational to avoid emotional intimacy. If you're someone who quickly dismisses another person because they're not intellectual or culturally sophisticated enough, you need to understand that this is your way of protecting yourself from closeness. I'm not suggesting that being interested in politics, the arts, culture, history or other pursuits isn't valuable and enriching. If you use such involvements to promote your superiority and denigrate those that are not intellectual and cultured, then the enrichment factor is also a defense against emotional closeness.

You may need to find someone who shares these interests but if your relationship is based on intellectual knowledge, you're not using your emotional brain which is what you need to have to express emotions, and what you need to feel close to someone.

You have to be asking yourself what am I feeling about this other person, not focusing on what great intellectual discussions you're having.

You'll have to learn and risk talking more about yourself, what you feel, care about and want you need from someone. You'll also have to risk becoming emotionally close, even to that person with whom you share intellectual interests.

8. Viewing Yourself as Superior

As a corollary to the intellectual defense thinking you are better than other people is a great distance regulator. It'll allow you to dismiss other people, denigrate people, and keep yourself safe in your superior bubble. If you do find someone who also thinks you are superior and feels fortunate to be with you, this kind of relationship isn't true intimacy. Being put on a pedestal by your spouse/partner doesn't allow for mutuality, essential for healthy intimate relationships. You may feel wonderful in the initial stage of your relationship but this won't last. Most long-term relationships even out the imbalance of superior/inferior. It's hard to remain the superior one when your partner has seen you naked, taking care of your bodily functions, and seeing all your flaws in the challenges of everyday living. You may be an expert in Constitutional Law but if you're unable to fix a leaky faucet or notice your wife's new hair style or are a poor lover, your superiority will wane over time.

So, you need to learn what constitutes true intimacy and let go of just using your rational or left brain. You need to ask yourself about your needs, wants and feelings and those of your partner. You'll have to go deeper into your relationship at an emotional level to discover how to find real intimacy.

Changing Unresolved/Disorganized Attachment

People with Unresolved/Disorganized Attachments have experienced trauma or significant loss as children and haven't resolved the effect on their personalities from the trauma. Such trauma can include physical, sexual abuse, severe neglect, witnessing domestic violence or experiencing and witnessing the violence of war or conflict. Children who lost parents either through death or abandonment also can be traumatized. Trauma can also result from natural disasters that happen worldwide. We are more aware of the effects of combat on military men and women who return from their military duty with PTSD. We now see the effects of international conflicts on children and families as experienced by Syrian refugees and other refugees.

I'm going to focus on Unresolved Adult Attachment as the result of early childhood abuse and neglect although other forms of trauma are also devastating for the issues of trust and security.

Although I'll offer some self-interventions for people with Unresolved Attachments, I do encourage adults who would apply this form of Attachment to themselves to seek help from a professional trained in Trauma. There is risk in exploring one's childhood trauma without professional help. There are triggers that may cause a trauma response or memories that may emerge that are overwhelming. An essential factor in resolving one's early childhood trauma is the need for a slow pace in uncovering the memories and having a balance between experiencing the emotions and understanding issues of responsibility and accurate reality. A Trauma Specialist will help create the safety and balance for the exploration of your trauma.

Children who were abused by a parent or caregiver are deeply confused about this experience and often develop Disorganized Attachment. Infants and children instinctively turn to their parent or caregiver if they experience fear or stress. If the caregiver is the source of this threat then the child doesn't know what to do. Some children will hit the parent to protect themselves. Others will do whatever is required to avoid the caregiver. And still others will freeze, not allowing themselves to feel anything. Such children do not have a set or organized way of responding to the fear. All of the mentioned strategies are equally valid forms of protection. It isn't an indication of more strength or confidence if the child fights back rather than becomes comatose like and does nothing. How a child reacts probably is related to constitutionality and the child's perception of what would be most protective. If the child perceives that the caregiver is stronger than him or her and there's no escape from the environment or place of the abuse, the child will simply freeze to survive what's happening to him or her. If the child does see a way to avoid the person or to escape, the child will do so. If the child believes they can fight back as a way of fending off the abuser, the child will do so.

Most children don't have one way of protecting themselves and will use different strategies or tactics depending on the nature of the abuse and the circumstances at the time.

For instance, I worked with a religious woman who had been sexually abused as a child by her father. He was a well-respected religious professional in his community. She was a shy compliant child who was perceived by her family as the quiet reliable one.

Initially when the grooming began with back rubs, the girl felt confused. She had learned that men do not touch females. However, her mother was aware of this behaviour and seemed to approve of it or did not stop it. When the touching became more sexual, involving touching her breasts, the girl felt frightened and more perplexed. Her initial response was to avoid her father. As her father became more insistent in finding her and forcing her to endure his touching, she felt more helpless and found herself not feeling her body. She continued to try to protect herself by locking her door. Eventually, her father was able to find her alone and exposed himself. This girl, so terrified, literally fainted. Her body protected her from his terrifying advance. Her father was equally frightened by her fainting and stopped his abuse of her.

He moved on to his next victim, his younger daughter. However, this girl was a very spunky outspoken girl who was also encouraged by her sister to report anything their father did to her that was uncomfortable and inappropriate. She reported to her sister that her father had touched her breasts. Eventually this man was reported to Child Welfare and was removed from his family.

My client used a number of strategies to avoid her father's abuse but never felt empowered to fight back or tell her mother. Her father was a powerful man in the family and community and so my client felt defenseless and unable to tell anyone what this perfect man was doing. Even after he was reported my client felt the need to protect him from the community's condemnation.

Children who've been abused or neglected often feel this happened because of something they did. They may also feel the sexual abuse places them in a special status with their father or caregiver. At other times the abuser has threatened that if they tell anyone the family will be destroyed or the father will go to jail or the child will be sent away.

If you've been abused as a child, your lack of protection has likely resulted in your seeing the world as an unsafe, if not very dangerous, place as an adult. You'll have great difficult trusting others and have many strategies to keep your distance from others. You may behave as a victim in relationships or as a perpetrator, each a result of your abusive childhood. You may find yourself remembering your abuse or feeling the effects of it by many experiences you have as an adult. Such feelings and memories may be stimulated by your senses, i.e. tasting, smelling, feeling or hearing something, by seeing a person that looks like your perpetrator, by sexual experiences or by behaviours in your partner or anyone else. Such stimulants are called triggers and may happen frequently or infrequently.

You'll need to explore your childhood experience, feel the pain of how badly you were treated, mourn for the loss of all the love and caring you wanted and deserved and come to understand how your childhood affected your personality. With this difficult process you can resolve the trauma of what happened to you as a child and emerge with Earned security. You'll have a childhood story that'll be sad and painful but you'll own your story without self-blame and shame.

In trying to change your Unresolved Attachment you need to take the following steps:

1. Understand without any reservation that you were not to blame.

Adults are fully responsible for the abuse or neglect of their children. Children are the victims, not in any way responsible or colluders in the abuse. This is true even if:

- Your body experienced pleasure during your parent's sexual abuse of you
- You didn't tell your parent to stop or tell someone what was happening
- You may have misbehaved before you were physically or sexually abused
- You may have neglected to do a chore or perform some duty before the abuse
- You may have misbehaved or not performed well at school or in the community before the abuse or neglect.
- You're told and believe that you're not pretty enough, not smart enough, not good enough
- You told your non-abusing parent or another adult who didn't believe you.
- You were made to feel special and were given gifts and privileges not offered to your siblings.

Whatever abuse happened in your family, foster home, institution, you'll need to message yourself that you were not to blame and that the adult or adults perpetrating the abuse were irresponsible caregivers and fully accountable in law and according to social moral standards for their abuse. Caregivers have the duty, if they don't have the instinct, to love and protect the children in their care. YOU WERE A VICTIM.

2. Understand the meaning of Trauma and Loss and its effects.

Trauma is an event or events that usually involve frightening experiences that one can't control and leaves one feeling helpless, vulnerable, and unsafe. When such experiences are a regular component of a child's life, such children may experience the world as an unsafe place and all adults as potentially dangerous. Children and adolescents who are disrespectful to teachers, police officers and other adults in authority positions may be children who were abused and do not trust such authority figures. Such children then become adults who continue to feel a lack of control in their personal lives, do not trust other adults and who expect to be treated poorly in life. They often are missing the internal strength to cope with life's challenges

You'll need to learn about the effects of trauma that continue into adulthood for adults with Unresolved Attachments and understand those that apply to you. Some of these are:

- You continue to feel powerless in adult relationships
- You may try and gain power by being manipulative and aggressive
- You continue to act as a victim and chose controlling aggressive partners
- You are sexually provocative both because you perceive yourself as a sexual object and this offers some control in relationships
- You continue to blame yourself for your childhood abuse
- You feel your body is damaged and you have a very negative body image.
- You may feel a deep sense of shame and worthlessness
- You do not trust your partner or spouse
- You may experience intrusive thoughts, have flashbacks about your childhood experiences, may have sleep disturbances and eating disorders
- Overall you feel disorganized inside yourself and don't understand why you feel so worthless and so emotionally unregulated

The most significant effect of your trauma in understanding your attachment is that you never feel the basic trust that comes with Secure Attachment and you continue a pattern in relationships of being victimized or being an abuser or both.

3. Understand your triggers in relationships and situations.

Sandra was a married woman with children who was aware of her childhood sexual abuse by a boarder in her home. She had tried to "put this behind her" and live a normal life. In many ways she was very successful but was easily angered by her husband. When she was angry she became very irrational, hurling insults at her husband, at times throwing things and more dangerously, at times leaving her husband and driving her car. She did not want to deal with her abuse fearing it would have only detrimental effects on her personal life and career.

One day Sandra arrived for her therapy with me completely emotionally wrought. She could barely speak. After doing some deep breathing and practicing some of our grounding techniques she was able to explain what happened. She'd been taking a shower and was washing her underarms with soap when she had a full blown anxiety attack and a flashback about being in her childhood home and knowing her abuser was entering her room.

I knew that her abuser had ejaculated in Sandra's orifices, such as her underarms, behind her knees and in her bent elbows. When I reminded Sandra about the nature of his abuse and that she must have felt a sticky and soapy sensation in these parts after the abuse, her experience in the shower made sense to her. "A light bulb went on," Sandra said and this awareness prevented any other similar triggers.

She was also able to recognize that some behaviours of her husband were also triggers, igniting her anger and need to flee from him. Any positive comment he made about her body or appearance was one trigger. Because she felt her body had aroused the perpetrator and had been damaged by the abuse she couldn't tolerate any remarks about her body. Once she and her spouse recognized this, they were able to discuss what he could and couldn't say when he wanted to compliment her.

You'll need to explore all the behaviours and responses from your partner or spouse that arouse intense feelings in you that you know are inappropriate for the situation or discussion. You'll also need to be aware of all the stimuli in your environment that bring back memories or intense reactions. Make a list of these so you can be aware of them and tell yourself that such behaviours, events, situations and sensations can no longer hurt you. They're reminders of when you were a helpless child. You're now an adult with far more internal and external supports and power.

4. Grounding yourself.

Similar to people with Anxious Attachments you'll need to learn techniques that help you regulate your emotions but also how to ground yourself in your present reality when you're triggered.

- Learn Yoga breathing techniques and use these when you feel yourself becoming overly anxious, angry, sad or fearful. Concentrating on your breathing will be difficult when your emotions are so intense but continue to practice this. You may want to take some yoga classes or other exercise practices that teach relaxation. Don't give up if it takes you some time to let your thoughts and feelings lessen in intensity and find the calm that comes from concentrated breathing.

- Grounding Techniques: If you're alone when the triggers are activated, you will need to focus on something benign or calming in your environment. Sometimes I help clients concentrate on the feeling he or she is experiencing by sitting in their chair: feeling their feet on the floor, their bum on the seat, their hands on their lap or the arms of the chair. They and you can find a picture on the wall and describe what you see. The idea is to ground yourself in the present so your memories of bad times don't overwhelm you and drag you back to that awful time. Stay present and figure out ways to help you do this.

- If you have a supportive spouse or partner and something they're doing or saying is triggering you, stay with him or her, tell him or her what you're experiencing and figure out together what would help you get grounded in the present. In time this will become easier for both of you. Remember it is helpful to your spouse or partner if they know you're having a difficult reaction because of your past not because of your present relationship. It's comforting and empowering for your partner or spouse to feel that they can help you feel better when you're so upset.

5. Acknowledging your Abusive Past

I am very reluctant to encourage people with Unresolved Attachments to explore their pasts without a therapist guiding and supporting them. I encourage you to find a therapist who does specialize in Trauma.

Similar to other people with other forms of Attachment, you'll have to explore your past, try and capture memories of your relationships with your parents or caregivers, however painful these may be. You'll need to create your life story from all your memories and understanding, including the painful childhood occurrences. Similar to doing this in therapy you'll have to go slowly so you're not overwhelmed by the memories and feelings they generate. The idea in remembering isn't to be flooded by your past but to understand it differently as an adult. If you become overwhelmed by feelings, you'll have to stop the exploration, ground yourself in the present, soothe yourself and focus on the positives in yourself. You can always resume your exploration at another time. It's inside you and not going anywhere.

Your goal is to remember, allow these memories to become part of your childhood experiences, know, as an adult, how innocent and vulnerable you were as a child, be clear in your mind that you were not responsible for the abuse or neglect and in time decide how you want to deal with the caregivers who abused you, if they're still alive. This decision is now in your control.

Present Relationships

If you chose your partner/spouse when your attachment category was insecure, you'll have to examine whether this relationship has the potential to meet your needs and wants as an Earned Secure Attached individual. Your newly Internalized Relationship Model will enable you to feel a healthy sense of entitlement to express your feelings, needs and wants. You'll be capable of reciprocity in the relationship with your spouse or partner each meeting the other's needs to a reasonable degree.

If you recognized that you have a **Preoccupied/Anxious Attachment**, you may have chosen a Dismissing/Avoidant person, believing he or she would be a strong, stable and available. As you change your perception, attitude and behaviour, becoming less demanding, less dependent and less anxious and angry, your present partner/spouse may:

- Respond very positively, relieved by the reduced emotionality and demands and become more available both emotionally and physically.
- Continue to be emotionally remote, rebuffing your legitimate and appropriate expression of feelings, needs and wants. You may realize your partner has significant problems in intimacy and either insist on couple therapy or his or her own therapy. You may conclude your partner/spouse will not change and decide to end the relationship.
- Be puzzled and mistrustful of the changes in you. You may need to reassure your partner/spouse that you're more self-aware of your contribution to the problems in the couple relationship and be understanding of your spouse's mistrust. You may need to offer more time to determine if your spouse can develop the trust and belief that you have changed. You may also need the time to determine if the relationship will also change so both your and your partner's needs are met.

If you determined that you have a **Dismissing/Avoidant Attachment** and are working on being more emotionally open, expressing your needs and wants and seeking closeness in relationships, you will have to examine your present relationship to determine:

- If your partner/spouse can tolerate and respond positively to your new capacity to express your feelings and needs. If you're partnered with a Preoccupied Person who is very dependent and demanding, he or she may be threatened by your new expectations for mutuality. You'll need to reassure your partner that your changes will allow you to meet more of his or her needs, but you will expect more of the same. If your partner isn't able to tolerate reciprocity in the relationship, you may have to consider therapy or termination of the relationship.

- If you're married or partnered with another Dismissing Person, you may need and want more intimacy than they're capable of. Without changing the dynamics in your present relationship you are vulnerable to reverting to your previous unhealthy position of avoiding intimacy and repressing your newly realized feelings and desire for closeness. You may again need to consider if this person is a healthy choice for you.

- If, as a Dismissing/Avoidant Attached person, you were a caregiver and chose a Disorganized Attached person that you wanted to rescue and protect or a person with other disabilities, you'll have to examine and discuss how you can maintain the relationship and still have more of your emotional needs met. You may not be able to terminate the relationship because of your guilt or legitimate care-giving responsibilities. You may have to consider developing a close friendship with someone outside your marriage to provide more of your needs. This isn't easy for men, in particular but it will be important that you have someone to share your feelings and concerns with. I am not referring to a sexual partner but a close friend.

If you determined that you are an **Unresolved/Disorganized** Attached adult with a history of trauma and loss but have resolved your issues of trauma through therapy or your own healing, you will also have to examine your present relationship.

If you chose a partner when you were still feeling responsible for your abuse, you may have chosen someone who also is abusive. You may have excused this abusive treatment with all kinds of rationales or believed that you deserved this bad treatment. Your newly discovered awareness and recovery from your trauma may result in your decision to leave your partner/spouse. As difficult as this may be, it may reflect your belief that you deserve a partner who treats you as an equal, with kindness and respect.

You may have a partner who has tolerated the ups and downs of your self-healing but has had enough and tells you he/she is leaving. You feel devastated and abandoned. You should certainly try and reassure your partner that your emotional swings are part of the healing process and will eventually be stabilized. This may be a time to see a professional therapist who can help your partner understand the effects of trauma and the journey of healing.

However, your partner may insist on leaving. If you're closer to the end of your trauma resolution and feeling more secure, you'll be able to manage the separation. You'll need to reassure yourself that you'll be fine on your own and eventually find a healthy partner to complement your own healthy sense of self.

Chapter 8

OTHER IMPORTANT
ATTACHMENT CONCEPTS

ɔɲ

This chapter will discuss two important concepts that are relevant to how we behave in adult relationships. They develop from how we are parented as young children but continue to deeply effect us as adults. I will discuss the concepts as normative processes in childhood, how they become harmful in our development and then offer exercises to change such negative effects in our adult selves and relationships.

Reprimand and Repair

It's inevitable that children will need to be reprimanded and have consequences applied for inappropriate behaviour. Children do need expectations, rules and routines for their own self-organization, to develop a sense of morality and to feel safe in their home environment. Having rules and expectations helps children learn right from wrong and helps them adapt and be successful in other social situations such as school, extracurricular activities and work. However, the application of rules and consequences needs to be done with both empathy and firmness, not in a punitive authoritarian manner. Children should not be fearful of their caregivers. They should be respectful of their caregivers and feel safe with them.

When we, as parents, reprimand our children we and they may feel a break in the loving connection we have. This is normal. If we are feeling annoyed or angry at our children for their misbehaviour or defiance of us we may not feel love and the desire to have fun with them. If our children are angry at us they also do not feel warm fuzzy feelings for us.

What is essential in this process of reprimand and consequences and feeling the disconnect is the repair or reconnection. Secure parents are able to feel angry at their child in the moment of scolding their child, and then let the anger go and reconnect with their child with love and caring. If children experience this dynamic of reprimand and repair, they recognize that they were being punished for their behaviour and not for being a bad child. If children don't experience the repair or reconnect, they feel they were bad children and continue to feel this core sense of shame.

Children raised in orphanages rarely experience the repair part of being punished. If they were challenging children, they may have been reprimanded and punished by one staff who wasn't available later on to resolve the issue and assure the child they were still loved and valued. A staff on a different shift may do the same scolding, again without repair. Such institutionalized children often feel they're bad or worthless and don't trust the adults to be loving and forgiving.

Children who had a parent who was abusive or punitive in a drunken or enraged state rarely experienced the repair as well. An abusive parent may never recover from the anger or not remember the abuse after a drunken period. Again, such children always feel fearful of the parent and maybe self-blaming but never experience the process of anger/ disconnect and love/connection.

If you have a parent who became angry at you based on their mood and feeling, not on your behaviour you may also feel they you were a bad child and not trust your parent to reconnect and express love and closeness. This may or may not happen based on the mood of your parent not on what you do.

If you had a parent who became angry and reprimanding because your performance wasn't good enough, you would only feel the love and connection if you improved your performance. You would come to believe that your parent's love and pride in you was based on being the best in your activity or performance and always feel a sense of shame that you're not good enough. You would always be anxious that you'll anger your parent and not be able to calm them and regain their love. No child can always be the best in what they do.

So how are childhood experiences of reprimand and repair significant for you as an adult? Let's say you experienced your parents/caregivers being angry at you for some unacceptable behaviour. They gave you consequences for this behaviour, but later they were able to talk to you about your actions and you felt they were back to a calm loving state. You, as an adult, will be able to tolerate anger and conflict with your partner/spouse, knowing that you'll be able to reclaim your loving and calm feeling. You'll know that the conflict is about a particular issue or behaviour and not related to you as a total person. Anger and conflict won't threaten your relationship so every time you have an argument you won't feel it means the end of your relationship. You'll trust yourself to be able to resolve the issue, regulate your anger and reclaim the love and affection between you and your partner/spouse.

If, on the other hand, your experience as a child was to have parents/caregivers who were angry and punitive without resolving issues and returning to a calm loving state, you'll feel that any conflicts or angry episodes with your spouse/partner or close friend are threatening to you and the relationship. During such conflicts you may become insecure, self-blaming, disorganized inside yourself, and fearful that your relationship is over. You may become desperate to reconnect with your spouse/partner, demanding reassurance he or she still love you. Or you may feel the need to protect yourself and create distance for long periods. It will be very difficult for you to initiate the repair in the relationship or trust that your partner/spouse is sincere if they try and do this.

So, think about what conflict in your intimate relationship means to you and try to understand this meaning and your reaction from your childhood experiences. Changing your fearful negative reaction involves understanding the concept of conflict, disconnect and reconnect. You must convince yourself that anger and conflict in a relationship are normal and not necessarily destructive to the relationship. Conflict usually involves a disagreement about an issue, a criticism about something one person did, or a feeling that your spouse or partner didn't understand you or meet your needs, or the inappropriate involvement from a family member. If you focus on the issue, the disagreement, your feelings and needs, or the involvement of an inappropriate family member you'll either be able to resolve this or agree to disagree without resentment and blame. What is most important is that the anger and feeling of disconnect from the conflict dissipates and you're able to feel love, affection and contentment for and with your partner/spouse.

EXERCISE

1. After an argument with your partner/spouse or close friend that leaves you feeling terrible and afraid that the relationship is over, take some time for yourself.

2. Think about your childhood and try to remember what happened when your parent or caregiver was angry at you.

3. Did your parent make up with you after an angry episode when you may have been punished? Did they stay angry and not talk about what happened, leaving you feeling badly about what you had done?

4. Realize that your childhood experience left you believing, in the present, that conflict in your intimate relationships could end the relationship. Realize that this is not necessarily the reality now for you.

5. Go back to your partner, spouse or friend and talk about the issue that created the conflict. Own your part in the conflict, apologize and try to reconnect with this person.

6. If your spouse/partner is not ready to make up, give him or her time to do this, assuring him or her that you understand and hope he or she will be able to do this in short period of time. Do not get angry again or take this personally. Everyone repairs the disconnect at his or her pace.

7. Try again to talk about the conflict soon if your partner cannot. You can be the one who does more of the repair.

Shame

Shame is the feeling that's generated in the child when there has been a prolonged rupture or disconnect between a parent and child and no repair. If the parent's anger has been out of control and the parent has engaged in verbally or physically abusive behaviour, the child will feel a poisonous disconnect that's destructive to the security and well being of the child. Such reaction on the part of the parent leaves the child feeling frightened, alone and rejected. The child feels a deep sense of shame. Shame involves the child feeling he or she is a terrible defective person. It isn't the behaviour that is the problem; it's the child.

If harmful unrepaired ruptures become the norm in parent child relationships, the child will internalize this feeling of shame or defectiveness. Such a feeling is so painful and soul destroying that the child will do everything to avoid the feeling. Shame becomes their ingrained belief about themselves and defending against this feeling becomes an automatic response.

In my work with Adopted children I would see the behaviour and attitude stemming from these feelings of shame. These children would blame everyone else for their difficult behaviour, deny they did anything wrong, blatantly lie and become aggressive. Such defenses only made people in their lives angrier at them, leaving them feeling even more alone and rejected. It is difficult for parents and other adults in their lives to understand that underlying the lying, denial and blaming others is a child who feels they are terrible human beings.

Remember Gregory, the boy who'd been adopted from an orphanage. He had a deep sense of shame and had a very difficult time taking responsibility for his difficult behaviour. Acknowledging he'd done something wrong made him feel so terrible that he denied it or became angry at his father. I recall one time in therapy his father reported that Gregory had stolen a $20 bill but dropped in on sidewalk as he was leaving his home to go to school. Gregory had deliberately dropped the money feeling very badly about taking it. He was anticipating reprimand by me and could not hear me praise him for not keeping the money. His shame didn't allow him to hear any positive feedback. I had to repeat my praise over and over again until he could accept that he himself had repaired the wrong he had done.

Children who remain in this state of shame and defensiveness become adults who are easily but unknowingly triggered into the state of shame. To quote Daniel Seigel:

> If we have repeated experiences of toxic rupture without repair in our own childhoods, shame may play a significant role in our mental lives, even outside our awareness. Sudden shifts in our feelings and in our communication with others may indicate that the shame defenses are becoming activated. Experiences in which we feel vulnerable or powerless can trigger the defenses that our minds have constructed to protect us from awareness of such a painful state of shame when we were children. (*Parenting from the Inside Out*, p. 197)

This shame in adults is easily activated by a rupture in their relationship with their partner or spouse. Even the slightest negative remark can trigger the defensive rage. Once activated it is very difficult for the shamed person to gain control of their emotions and recognize that their reaction is based on distorted perceptions. Even kindness and reassurance by the other is ineffective once a person feels shame and humiliation.

Sandra, whom I mentioned in previous chapters, had been sexually abused as a young child and never told her parents or any other adults. She internalized a belief that she was at fault and that her body was damaged. She had other medical problems that involved invasive surgery, adding to her experience of a flawed body. As an adult Sandra fluctuated from admiring her body to hating it. She dressed according to her state at the time, loose clothing when the shame was prevalent and more fitting clothes when she was secure about her body. She married a man who was in love with her and found her very attractive. He did eventually learn of the abuse but didn't understand its impact on her.

When she was in her state of shame and body deprecation, she could not tolerate praise. She would tell her husband that she believed she looked terrible. He would try and assure her that she looked wonderful and encouraged her to buy or wear clothes that were more flattering. His praise only enraged her more which left him confused and helpless. In therapy she was able to understand her own body distortion and tell her husband that she needed him to be empathic, not try and change her view of her body. He finally understood that all he could do was tell her he understood how much she hated her body at that moment and was there anything he could do to help.

If you feel your childhood experiences have left you with this deep-seated feeling of shame, there are interventions you can use to heal this feeling, develop greater self-worth, and come to believe you're a person worthy of love, respect and appreciation. We've covered some of these in the previous chapters but I will both repeat some highly relevant ones and offer some self-interventions specific to healing shame.

---

1. The first step in recovering from your shame is to understand that you hold a deep but distorted and wrong belief that you're a flawed and terrible human being. You came to believe this because of your negative childhood experiences that involved ruptures, blame, criticism, punishment, and/or abuse. All of these negative experiences occurred without any resolve or without your parent reconnecting with you after such parental rejection. You were not a bad child and you are not a bad adult. Without this self-awareness and honest looking at yourself, you won't change.

2. Be aware of the triggers that arouse your feelings of shame. This can be criticism from your partner/spouse or anyone that you value, feelings of abandonment if your partner must be absent for a time for legitimate reasons or needs his or her own space, being less than perfect in your performances, activities or work and many other situations or sensations.

3. The biggest challenge for you will be to stay with the shameful feeling rather that use your old defenses. You may need to distance yourself from the trigger to do this or just spend some time alone allowing this painful feeling.

4. If you do use your defensive ways of suppressing the shame, such as getting angry, denying you did something, blaming someone else, or other actions, then understand that it was too difficult in that moment to feel your shame. But talk to the person you distanced with your defenses once you are calmer and mindful, explain your understanding of what happened, apologize if necessary and own your part in the dynamic.

5. Healing your feelings of shame can happen only in a very trusting relationship with someone who understands that you feel you're a deeply flawed human being. If you're in a relationship in which your partner has shown you

that he or she can be understanding and trustworthy then share this reality about yourself. If you come to believe that you're in a relationship in which your partner/spouse confirms for you that you're a bad person, then you'll need to examine if this relationship is going to contribute to your healing.

6. I would suggest if this is the case you seek professional help to explore your present relationship to determine if this is someone you should leave or someone that would be open to change. The most important intervention for your recovering from your deep-seated feelings of shame is to be kind to yourself and ensure you stop your self-criticism, your need to be perfect and running from the feelings of badness. You will have to be your own good parent, offering yourself comfort, support, soothing, nurturing and realistic praise.

Chapter 9

ADULT ATTACHMENT
AND PARENTING

$\mathcal{O}$

Perhaps one of the most important reasons that we should work on ourselves to redevelop Secure Attachment is for our children. There's very clear evidence that our Adult Attachments get passed on to our children because of how we parent them. This means that the issues from childhood that you're not aware of or haven't resolved will influence how you interact with and respond to your children. Your Insecure Adult Attachment, without your conscious awareness will be recreated in your child.

I mentioned in Chapter 3 that my mother had experienced an abusive and neglectful childhood, filled with poverty and a mean father. Her mother had been loving but so abused and poor that she had little to offer her children. My mother came to believe that she had to take care of herself, that she couldn't trust others, particularly men, and that being vulnerable and emotional was dangerous. How did she pass this on to me? Both directly and unconsciously. She very much wanted children and particularly a daughter. She wasn't a warm affectionate woman or mother and I learned early that she wouldn't offer me comfort or warmth if I was emotionally upset. When I grew older, she would tell me directly not to ask others for help or for anything as I'd then be dependent on them or beholding in some way. She passed on her beliefs about relationships and wasn't capable of emotional availability herself. Yet, she very much wanted me to find happiness with a man, since she hadn't, and couldn't understand why I had such difficulty doing this. I had developed a Dismissing Adult Attachment because of her parenting. Neither she nor I understood this when I was a young adult.

Another example of how parents react based on their Adult Attachment is from an adoptive family that I worked with many years ago before I understood and focused on Adult Attachment. The child was four years old when he was adopted and was traumatized from his experiences of being neglected as an infant and removed from a caring foster home. His adoptive parents were not warm and affectionate, which they acknowledged. They were very knowledgeable of the effects on adopted children from being neglected and rejected and understood intellectually what their son needed. They worked very hard with me but this boy didn't change much. There was an emptiness inside him that he tried to fill by stealing, developing superficial relationships and clinging to his adoptive parents. He couldn't focus on school, homework or chores and wasn't able to develop healthy peer relationships. The parents were more concerned about his performance in school and his difficult behaviour rather than his emotional deprivation and need for nurturing and love from them.

The parents became angry and rejecting of this boy although they understood his terrible history. As children these parents had been very good and obedient and became successful adults in their professions. They were not used to feeling incompetent and rather than opening up about these vulnerable feelings, the adoptive father worked more and was more absent and the mother read more about parenting strategies for troubled adoptive children. I couldn't find my way into their emotions and help them be more empathic to the sadness and pain of this boy. They and I failed to connect to the underlying fear of closeness this boy had.

I now understand that both parents were Dismissing Attached Adults who had great difficulty expressing their own needs and emotions and who focused on achievement and success. I wish I had helped them understand this so they could have understood that their lack of connection to their adoptive child was coming from their own emotional limitations. If they had understood this and worked on their own Attachment styles, they would've been able to emotionally connect to the inner world of their son.

A more recent case I was working with involves a family with two adopted boys. They were challenging because of their early history and because of some genetic factors that each inherited. Both parents were devoted and very involved but tended to focus on rules and behaviour. They know from their work with me that they need to be empathic to their children rather than so angry and authoritative. The mother had a difficult time with this. In my work with her she acknowledged how hard it was for her to understand their defiance of rules and difficulty focusing on school and chores. She had been a well behaved child who would never defy her parents. She was also an excellent student who valued learning and getting good marks. Why couldn't her children be like this?

There's an excellent book called *Parenting from the Inside Out* by Dan Seigel and Mary Hartzell. What does "parenting from the inside out" mean? I'm sure many of you reading this book have taken parenting courses or read books on parenting and learn methods or philosophies of parenting. One can learn and practice methods of parenting. These are often hard to do because our emotions and the way we were parented get in the way. So if you're parenting from learning the outside methods and not dealing with what's inside of you, you'll continue to parent your children as you were parented in spite of your determination to learn proper parenting.

I remember one time that my daughter said to me "you sound just like Baba." I was being anxious and controlling and demanding some behaviour from my child. It was a startling reminder that I could be just like my mother in my parenting if I was unaware of what I was doing. Not that all her parenting was bad and not that I shouldn't emulate some of how she raised me. The parenting behaviour that I was showing my daughter wasn't what I wanted to duplicate from my mother.

There are also excellent books on Attachment Focused Parenting that I highly recommend. Dan Hughes and Arthur Becker Weidman are two specialists in Attachment Focused Parenting who have well researched and methods that one should practice as a parent.

I want to focus on what your tendencies or vulnerabilities are as a parent based on the type of Adult Attachment you have.

Preoccupied (Anxious/Ambivalent)

If you're an adult with a Preoccupied/Anxious Attachment, your challenge as a parent is being consistently available to your child and not expecting your child to meet your emotional needs. Remember, as a Preoccupied Adult you have difficulty trusting others and are highly sensitive to someone not being available to meet your needs. This sensitivity also may involve your parenting. You may understand that your children are not in this world to meet your needs but practicing this will be difficult for you. By the time you're reading this book your child may already be challenging and demanding of your attention in unhealthy ways. Remember your child may have learned that the best way to get your attention is to be demanding and dramatic. Your child may also become enraged at you when you're not paying attention to him or her, even when this may be for legitimate reasons.

If your child is already challenging both with his or her anger and manipulative behaviour, you may be feeling inadequate as a parent and angry at your child for making you feel this way. This feeling of inadequacy may result in your withdrawing from your child and ignoring their demands. If this is the case, I would bet your child becomes more demanding and clinging and trying all kinds of behaviour to get your attention. They may become nicer and more loving. If this doesn't work to get your attention they may pretend to be sick. They'll try whatever works to pull you back into a relationship with him or her.

The following are what you need to work on as a parent with a Preoccupied Attachment while you're working on yourself:

1. Do not personalize your infants or child's more challenging behaviour. If your baby is fussy and not easy to settle, stay calm, tell yourself this is not your fault and your baby may be having a difficult time because of gas problems, breast feeding problems or just adjusting to being out of your safe and warm stomach. Your baby may need time to adjust or even time to develop more sucking skills or digestive maturity. If you do find yourself, becoming angry and rejecting of your baby, find someone to help you and let you have a break. Use this break to talk to yourself and control your anger. Do this in as short a time as you can manage. It is important that you learn you can manage your insecurity as a parent and not be dependent on others on a regular basis. Becoming a first time parent is a major challenge and be kind to yourself in learning how to be the best parent you can be.

2. The challenge for you with your older school age children is being consistent in your emotional availability. I know that your moods can be up and down and this will affect your parenting. When you are worried about your partner/spouse or angry at your own mother or

father or both, you are probably not attuned to the needs and feelings of your children. If you cannot get yourself out of your upset mood or preoccupation with your partner/spouse or whomever is upsetting you then tell your child/ren that you are not in a good mood and are sorry you cannot be playful with them or even spend quality time with them. It is important that your children do not feel that it is their fault you are in a bad mood. If necessary find someone to help you manage your children or again give yourself a break to get emotionally calm.

3. If you are feeling that your anger is getting so intense that you may hit your children or punish them in an extreme way, you must take a break from your children. If your children are old enough, leave them in a separate area in your home and go to another room and do whatever it takes to calm yourself. If your children are too young for this, then call someone you trust and have them come over to give you the break you need. Even if this is someone, like your mother, that you don't fully respect or trust, they may be better for your child or children for a short period while you relax.

4. Being consistent, thoughtful and taking responsibility for your feelings and behaviour will be your greatest challenge as a parent. If you own this and do not blame your children and others for your anxiety and anger you will be making a great step toward change.

5. Continue to practice all the techniques we discussed in chapter 7 to get your emotions under control and feel calmer. These include deep breathing, meditation, leaving the upsetting situation and talking to people you know will be supportive and help you calm down.

Dismissing/Avoidant Attachment

If you placed yourself in the Dismissing Category of Adult Attachment, your challenges as a parent usually involve needing to be a perfect parent and being too rational and demanding of the performance or the best behaviour from your child. This means that your child or children may not be able to be in touch with or express their needs, wants and feelings to you, similar to what happened to you as a child. You need to figure out what you expect of your child that isn't healthy for them.

Some parents with a Dismissing Attachment want their children to be happy and or at least be pleasant all the time and never express anger, sadness, pain or fear, what are sometimes called negative emotions. These are normal feelings that all human beings have at times and need to express. I told you about a client I had that learned this and so could never tell his parents when he was physically hurt and needed comfort and certainly couldn't express any deeper emotions like sadness or anger. He continued to be this easy-going pleasant man even in his marriage without any capacity for true intimacy. In time his wife felt the marriage was superficial and felt she never got to know her husband and what he was feeling. She left him wanting and needing more.

Other parents with Dismissing Attachment are narcissistic and self-serving and need their children to take care of them or make them look good to others. We all know parents who demand that their children are the best hockey players, get the best grades at school or be the best in whatever their children take on. These parents also demand that their children get involved in activities that the parent values or that the parent wished they had excelled at. These are activities that their children may not be interested in or not good at but the wants, feelings and strengths of the child or children don't count.

If you find yourself getting angry at your child for not being the best academically, not getting the best marks, not being the best hockey player, football player, swimmer, ballet dancer, piano player or whatever activity they're engaged in, you have to stop and ask yourself if this is for your needs and status. It's fine to encourage your child to be the best they can at school or in an activity they chose to try but your encouragement must be to make your child feel good about himself or herself, not for your personal needs or social status.

Some Dismissing Attached parents are very authoritarian, demanding obedience and respect from their children. I'm not suggesting that children be disobedient or disrespectful but all children at times challenge the authority of their parents and secure parents can normalize this and deal with this appropriately. Dismissing Attached parents become extremely angry and even abusive if their children question the rules and regulations or the expectations from the parent. Such parents definitely become enraged if their children become defiant of them or refuse to be the best in school and in their extracurricular activities. In this state of rage the Dismissing Parent may reject their child and withdraw from him or her or become physically abusive.

The greatest challenge for you if you're a parent with a Dismissing Adult Attachment is to allow yourself to be an imperfect parent who may at times feel inadequate and need to rely on others to help you or give you advice. Every parent needs to understand there are times when parenting is a frustrating experience that leaves you feeling unsure of yourself and puzzled by the behaviour of your child. Parenting can be a humbling experience that can allow you to grow and learn more about yourself or can be a humbling experience that makes you angry at your children. I hope you'll be able to learn from your children and allow yourself to feel unconditional love for them and for yourself.

The following are some guidelines to help you be the kind of parent that will raise a secure child and not another generation of Avoidant Children.

1. Allow yourself to feel incompetent, helpless, and needy of others and scared that you may not always know how to handle your children. If you can stay with these feelings and not bury them immediately or get angry at your children for arousing these feelings you will in time be able to tolerate them more and learn from them. Tell yourself that such feelings are normal for most parents and you can be one of the normal parents, not the perfect one.

2. Do not personalize your child's successes and particularly their poor performances. If your child is struggling in school or with their extracurricular activities, be curious, non-judgemental and empathic to your child. Tell your child that you can see that they are struggling, ask what is making the subject or activity hard for them and how you can help. You may need to speak to a teacher, a coach or instructor to get more information about your child's struggles. You can only do this if you're going to be open-minded and not ready to criticize and attack.

3. Be prepared to accept your child's different interests, abilities and pace. You may love hockey and were a great player in your youth, but your child may be interested in acting or music or some activity that doesn't interest you at all. Or you may find yourself attending every hockey practice and game when this is the last thing you want to be doing. Being a parent means you take an interest in your child's interests and skills. You do not impose your interests or your unmet dreams for your success on your child.

4. If you have a child, biological, foster, or adopted, with significant challenges, be ready to feel helpless and maybe at times a personal failure. I've worked with adopted parents with Dismissing Attachments and know how difficult it is for them to accept that they may not be able to change their child in the time they determined this change should have happened. Adopted children in particular take a long time to develop

trust and let go of the strategies they developed in orphanages or abusive homes to feel safe and get their needs met. You may read all the manuals on parenting and believe you're very knowledgeable about your child's particular challenge and still feel you're not helping or changing your child.

5. I worked with a mother who had an autistic child. She read every book and article on Autism, went to conferences and hired the best behavioural therapists to work with her child. She was an Adult with a Dismissing/Avoidant Attachment, who had a cold exceptionally beautiful mother and demanding abusive father. She tried to remain understanding and accepting of her son but when he wasn't progressing as she hoped, she became angry at him and his workers. When I explored with her both the limitations of herself and that of her son, she became extremely sad and began to cry. She was able to recognize that she had never mourned her loss and longing for a normal child. She was also able to recognize that she still had the desire to please her father either by having a normal child or producing the best functioning autistic child. Once this mother could accept her helplessness to produce such a son and accept that both she and her son were doing the best they could, she became more loving and playful with her son and kinder to herself.

6. Ask for support and guidance. You do not have to know it all and rely only on your own competencies. You may need to ask other parents how they manage similar challenges. You may need to seek help from an expert in parenting or in your child's particular challenge.

7. Parents with Dismissing Attachments sometime have a difficult time working with their spouse or partner and believe they know best. If you find yourself becoming angry at your partner/spouse because he or she doesn't follow your way of parenting, pause and consider that your way may not be the best. This is particularly the case if you've married or partnered with someone more emotional and softer in her parenting style. You'll have a difficult time with this approach believing that your spouse is spoiling your child or making them weak and not successful.

Be open to your partner's perception of your child and their ideas on how to parent. Your child will only benefit if you and your partner/spouse work together and find ways to compromise or at least be respectful of differences in parenting styles.

Parents with Unresolved Adult Attachments

If you discovered that you're a person with an Unresolved/Disorganized Adult Attachment, parenting may trigger many feelings and reactions from your past that you have not resolved. If you're to be the best parent you can be, you must work on resolving what happened to you as a child, as challenging as this may be. Parents with Unresolved/Disorganized Adult Attachments can be very frightening and unpredictable to their children. As a Parent with an Unresolved Adult Attachment you may feel that your moods shift without your knowing why or when your children's behaviour makes you angry for no logical reason. You may also find yourself spacing out when you can't manage your child or your child is stressed by something happening in their life.

Your unpredictable behaviour will be frightening and upsetting to your child. Perhaps your child will try and appease you to make you less angry, perhaps your child will avoid you just to escape your frightening behaviour and feelings, or your child may get angry back at you, making the situation worse. However your child reacts to you, your child will not be feeling safe and secure in his or her relationship with you.

I have used Marjorie as an example of an Unresolved Adult Attachment. When Marjorie was able to accept that her father had been an abuser and she his victim she could begin to examine what had happened to him that may help understand his abusive behaviour. Her father had a difficult childhood but his abusive behaviour had escalated after he returned from the war. He clearly had returned with Post Traumatic Stress Disorder. His behaviour was unpredictable. Some days he could be kind and loving to his children, other days he would be screaming at them and physically abusive, other days he would be withdrawn and uncommunicative and other days he would be drunk. Marjorie never knew when she returned from school which father she would encounter, the one who was kind to her or the one who demanded she come to his bedroom where he would sexually abuse her. Her father never dealt with his PTSD and at the time he returned from World War Two PTSD wasn't recognized or treated. His children, including Marjorie, also developed Unresolved Adult Attachments because of the frightening and confusing behaviour they experienced from their father. And because they weren't protected by their mother or other family members.

What can you do to ensure you don't pass on your Unresolved/Disorganized Attachment to your children?

1. Own it! What do I mean by this? If you know that you overreact to your children's behaviour you have to accept that the problem is you, not your children. If you find yourself getting angry when your child is doing something annoying or just being childlike, count to 100 before reacting. If you know that you have reacted inappropriately to your child's behaviour, tell your child that you're not in a good mood and apologize. Even if you do this a little later after you have over reacted, it'll help your child not blame him or herself and not be so afraid of you.

2. Learn the behaviours and feelings from your child that are triggers for you. These can be:
   - A child being defiant when this may be normal or an indication of your child having a difficult time. This may make you feel not

in control or frightened by the power of your child or rejected by your child.

- Your child being upset by some event or relationship in his or her life, such as school or peers that are being mean or rejecting. This may remind you of your own childhood experience and you may not be able to be empathic or helpful to your child.

- Your child being happy and showing this by skipping along, singing, being playful or laughing. If you're in a dark mood you may resent your child's happiness, or not be able to join in your child's pleasurable mood. You may become angry at your child and destroy their happy playful mood.

- Your child needing and wanting to be with you when you're feeling overwhelmed by other events in your life that have nothing to do with your child. You may be feeling the need to withdraw and be left alone, when your child is asking for attention. You may react in anger or just ignore your child and withdraw to your room, leaving your child feeling ignored and rejected.

- Any normal sexual behaviour your child demonstrates. It's normal for our children to self-sooth by touching or rubbing their genitals. If you were sexually abused as a child this may trigger your irrational fears that your child has been abused or will become an abuser. You may overreact by intensely questioning your child about who abused them or demand in an aggressive manner that they stop their behaviour. Shaming your child isn't helpful in redirecting them to a private area or other activities.

- Any intense feeling or reaction that you display that rationally you know is too extreme for what your child or children are doing should tell you that this is coming from an unresolved area of your life.

It is also not healthy or helpful for children to witness your anger and unpredictable behaviour toward your spouse or partner, particularly if this is the father or mother of your child. Lots of children have told me how frightening it is to hear their parents fighting, particularly if physical abuse is involved.

I worked with a family a number of years ago who was referred to the agency where I worked. The child who was the "problem" was a four-year-old girl who was displaying very concerning behaviour at school. She would be "spaced out" in the classroom and at recess would be found either wondering around or trying to go home. Initially I wondered if this child had been abused. Her parents were separated and the father was not allowed contact with his wife because of his abusive behaviour toward her. The mother assured me that her husband didn't come to the house and the children would visit him for their access. She clearly cared about her children, ensured they were well taken care of and seemed motivated to get her daughter the help she needed.

In the family meeting with the mother and her three children, two daughters, four and five years of age and a son, two, the children played with toys while we talked about their parents' separation and their feelings about this. Initially all the children denied that their father came to their house. I noticed that the two-year-old had an adult male in his play and I asked him about this. He told me that the male was his father who was upstairs in his house. Then the four-year-old also told me that her father was frequently at their house and she could hear them "correlling." She believed that she could control her father by telling him to stop. He would listen to her. The problem for this child was when she was at school. She knew that her father would come to the house in the daytime and she couldn't protect her mother. She sat in school worried about her mother and wanting to go home to stop the conflict. She couldn't concentrate on school and looked "spaced out" because she was preoccupied with worry for her mother.

This is a child who was traumatized by the conflict with her parents and her fear that her father would abuse her mother. She had witnessed this and became the child who would protect her mother and stand up to her father. She already had a Disorganized Attachment and without our intervention would have become an Unresolved Adult Attachment. The therapy focused on empowering this mother and helping her resolve her issues from an abusive childhood. We also challenged this father to abide by the restraining order. This little four-year-old was freed up from her protective role in the family and able to concentrate on school.

If you know that you have an Unresolved/Disorganized Adult Attachment, it's imperative that you focus on understanding what happened to you as a child, understand the impact that your abuse or neglect or loss had on you, recognize your triggers and then do everything you can to ensure that you do not continue to be a victim and repeat the abuse or neglect with your children. You will have to ensure that you become a survivor who can remember what happened to you, tell your story, know the setbacks and strengths you have developed because of your childhood history and become a more secure adult and parent.

As I mentioned in Chapter 7, I would recommend that you engage in therapy with a therapist who specializes in Trauma. Such a therapist can guide you through the process so you can resolve your childhood trauma and become a more secure parent who will raise secure children.

Chapter 10

CONCLUSIONS

This book has focused on a way of understanding and transforming yourself based on a theory called Attachment.

When a child is born an important process begins that will influence the child for a lifetime. This process is called Attachment. Attachment is the development of a deep and enduring connection between an infant and caregiver, usually a biological mother. The infant communicates his or her needs, such as anger, discomfort, tiredness or stress and pleasure to the mother through behaviours such as crying, cooing, smiling and movement of arms and legs. If the mother or caregiver is sensitive to the needs of the infant and responds with consistency and caring, the infant will develop a healthy and secure attachment to the caregiver. If the caregiver doesn't respond to the needs of the infant, responds in unpredictable ways or worse, neglects or hurts the infant, the infant will develop an insecure attachment or connection to the caregiver.

Similar to childhood, adults want to be understood, find support and feel nurtured in their close relationships. However, whether an adult will be able to achieve this in a healthy manner will depend on the combination of early attachment experiences plus the failures or successes in relationships in childhood and adolescence. Adults who had caring

parents or caregivers and continued to seek and find positive relationships in adolescence will have secure relationships as an adult. Those
adults who had poor early caregiving experience and continued to
develop impoverished relationships in childhood and adolescence will
have deprived adult relationships.

The first chapter of this book described the types of Adult Attachment
and how to recognize the type or types that best describe how you see
yourself and how you behave in relationships. What is also crucial in
determining your Attachment Style is how you remember your childhood and understand the impact your childhood experience has on
your present behaviour and self-perception as an adult.

For many people learning about Adult Attachment and seeing yourself
as a certain type is an 'ah-ha experience.' You may have been aware of
difficulties in relationships, have been told by others, including your
parents, friends, partners and spouses about your attitudes and behaviours that pose challenges. You may have been in therapy before reading this book and had some awareness about yourself. You may have
found your therapy to be helpful or not or somewhere in between. But
now you have a new way of perceiving your challenges and hopefully
with a non-judgemental approach.

You may have been aware that you're a workaholic, always focussed
on achieving and being the best in whatever endeavour you take on.
You may have some awareness that you feel anxious when people try
to get too personal with you and certainly when your spouse/partner
complains that you aren't emotionally available. You may wish your
children talked to you more but know how awkward you feel if they
turn to you for emotional support. Now you have a means of understanding yourself that makes sense. Whether you're able to change your
personality, you at least understand how your personality developed

and have a greater appreciation for the people in your life that miss your emotional involvement.

You may also be aware that you're very emotional, get very upset when your spouse/partner works long hours or has to go out of town for his/her job. You know it will annoy him/her but can't stop yourself from calling him/her many times in the day. At times you're convinced he/she is having an affair or lying to you, and these thoughts preoccupy you so you're unable to concentrate on anything else, including paying attention to your children. You have told yourself not to confront your spouse/partner when he/she comes home but have lost it as soon as you saw him/her, yelling, crying, attacking and demanding reassurance. You believe you'll do this again although you have tried to stop.

Hopefully the description of Preoccupied/Anxious Attachment has helped you understand that you're hyper sensitive to issues of separation, abandonment and unavailability because of the inconsistent parenting your received. Being emotionally balanced is a challenge for you and an area you'll need to work on. Hopefully also you now understand your Attachment Category with a kind and a non-judgemental self-regard.

This nonjudgement is what is so attractive and helpful in an Adult Attachment approach to understanding yourself. You came to be the way you are because of your early childhood experiences. Your parents parented the way they did because of their early childhood experience. You may be parenting in a similar manner because of your Adult Attachment. Your present way of parenting may not be helpful to developing secure children

You now have an opportunity to change your Adult Attachment so you can feel better about yourself, have healthier relationships, have better self-control or the opposite, more spontaneity and emotionality. This change will also break the cycle of poor parenting so your children can be more secure.

This book has offered practical guides and interventions for you to begin the process of change. Some interventions are generic and apply to all of the Attachment Categories and others are specific to your particular Attachment.

Change is not easy. By adulthood the patterns that we display in relationships to create closeness and distance are deeply entrenched. As the chapter on the brain showed us, our attachment patterns are deeply embedded in the part of the brain called the limbic system. We're usually not conscious of these patterns and therefore continue to repeat them in all our close relationships. Many of you understand what I mean. You left one partner and discovered that the next one who seemed so different was just like the first and maybe others from your past as well. Your unconscious or unaware self dominated your choice in spite of your conscious determination to find someone different.

However, if you make that unconscious part of your brain conscious you can make healthier choices in your relationships. The adult brain allows us to think about what we're doing, to understand its origins, to decide that certain patterns aren't healthy for us or the people we care about and to risk making changes in ourselves and in our relationships. With this change will come a new feeling of security. You'll feel good about yourself, choose relationships that support this good feeling and pass this security and positive self-regard onto your children.

Although the book has offered a new way of understanding yourself through an Attachment lens and self-help techniques to transform some of your patterns, you may need to consider psychotherapy so a professional therapist can guide you from insecurity to security. As I mentioned earlier in the book finding an Attachment Focused Therapist may be difficult but any good therapist who understands the need to develop a trusting relationship with his or her client and to examine the past as it lives on in the present will be helpful.

There's a funny cartoon from *The New Yorker* that I use in my training on Adult Attachment. It shows a typical therapist and client and the caption reads: "You're born, you deconstruct your childhood and then you die." There's a large segment of reconstruction left out after you deconstruct your childhood and before you die. I suggest that this reconstruction allows you to live a full life where you'll have healthy mutual relationships, where you'll feel worthy of love and respect and where you'll pass on the love and respect to the generations that follow.

BIBLIOGRAPHY

Books

Arden, John, *Rewire Your Brain*, (2010) New Jersey John Wiley and Sons

Atkinson, Leslie & Zucher, Kenneth J. *Attachment and Psychopathology.* (1997), New York, NY, Guilford Press

Becker-Weidman, Arthur, *Creating Capacity for Attachment*, 2008, Centre for Family Development, Buffalo, New York

Bennett, Susanne, Nelson, Judith Kay, *Adult Attachment in Clinical Social Work*, (2011), New York, Springer

Bowlby, John , *A Secure Base*, (1988), New York, NY: Basic Books

Brown, Daniel, P. & Elliot, David, *Attachment Disturbances in Adults* (2016) New York, W.W. Norton & Company

Busch, Karl Heinz, *Treating Attachment Disorders,* (2002), New York, Guilford Press

Cassidy, J. & Shaver, P.R. ed. *Handbook of Attachment*, (1999), New York, Guilford Press

Cassidy, J. & Shaver, P.R, ed. *Handbook of Attachment*, (Third Edition), (2018) New York, Guilford Press

Couttender, P. M. & Ainsworth, M, "Child Maltreatment & Attachment Theory," (1989), in *Child Maltreatment*, Cicchetti, Dante & Carlson, Vicki, New York, NY, Cambridge University Press.

Cozolino, Louis, *The Neuroscience of Human Relationships* (2006) New York, W.W. Norton & Co.

Daniel, Sarah, *Adult Attachment Patterns in a Treatment Context,* (2015) New York, Routledge

Doidge, Norman, *The Brain that Changes Itself,* (2007) New York, Penguin Books

Heller, Diane Poole, Levine, Peter, *The Power of Attachment: How to Create Deep and Lasting Relationships.* (2019)

Hesse, Erik, "The Adult Attachment Interview, Historical & Current Perspectives," in Cassidy & Shaver, *Handbook of Attachment* (1999), New York, Guilford Press, p. 395-433

Hughes, Daniel, *Attachment-focused Parenting,* (2009) New York, W.W. Norton & Co.

Hughes, Daniel, *Attachment Focused Family Therapy,* (2007) New York, W.W. Norton & Co.

Johnson, S. & Whiffen, V., *Attachment Processes in Couple and Family Therapy,* (2006) New York, Guilford Press

Johnson, Sue, Dr., *Hold Me Tight,* (2008) New York, Little, Brown & Co.

Kerns, Kathryn & Richardson, Rhonda, *Attachment in Middle Childhood,* (2005), New York, Guilford Press,

Levine, Amir & Heller Rachel S.F., *Attached* (2011) New York, Penguin Group

Milkulincer, Mario & Shaver, Phillip R, *Attachment in Adulthood,* (2016), New York, Guilford Press

Muller, Robert, *Trauma and the Avoidant Client,* (2010) New York, W.W. Norton & Co.

Obegi, Joseph and Berant, Ety, *Attachment Theory and Research in Clinical Work with Adults,* (2009) New York, Guilford Press

Sable, Pat, *Attachment and Adult Psychotherapy,* (2000), New Jersey, Jason Aronson Inc.

Siegel, Daniel, *Mindsight,* (2010) New York, Bantam Books

Siegel, Daniel & Hartzell, Mary, *Parenting from the Inside Out,* (2003), New York, Penguin Books

Siegel, Daniel, *The Mindful Brain* (2007) New York W.W. Norton and Co.

Siegel, Daniel, *The Whole-Brain Child*, (2011) New York, Delacorte Press

Simpson, Jeffery & Rhodes, W. Steven, *Attachment Theory and Close Relationships*,(1998) New York, Guilford Press,

Steele, Howard & Steele, Miriam, *Clinical Applications of the Adult Attachment Interview*, (2008), New York, Guilford PressTatkin, Stan, *Wired for Love*, (2011) Oakland, Cal. New Harbinger Publications Inc.

Wallin, David, *Attachment in Psychotherapy*, (2007) New York, Guilford Press

Articles

Edelstein, Robin, Alexander, Kristen Weede, Shaver, Phillip, Schaaf, Jeenifer,, Quas, Jodi, Lovas, Gretchen & Foodman, Fail, "Adult Attachment Style and parental responsiveness during a stressful event," in *Attachment & Human Development*, Volume 6, Issue 1, March 2004, pg. 21

Firestone, Lisa, "How Your Attachment Style Impacts Your Relationship," *Psychology Today*, Posted online July 30, 2013

Holmes, Jeremy, "Disorganized Attachment and Borderline Personality Disorder," in *Attachment and Human Development*, Volume 6, no. 2, June 2004

Kaitz, Marsha, Bar-Haim, Yair, Lehrer and Ephraim Grossman, "Adult attachment style and interpersonal distance," in *Attachment and Human Development*, Volume 6, No.3, Sept 2004, pg 285-304

Levy, Kenneth, & Johnson, Benjamin, "Attachment and Psychotherapy: Implications from Empirical Research," *Canadian Psychology*, 2018, Advance online publication

Main, M, Kaplan, N, Cassidy, J., 1987, "Security in Infancy, Childhood & Adulthood, A Move to the Level of Representation," in Bretherton & Waters, E. Eds. *Growing Points in /Attachment Theory and Research Monogram of Society for Research, Child Development* 5.0 (1-2) p 66-104

O'Sullivan, Patrick, "Breaking Away, A Harrowing True Story of Resilience, Courage and Triumph," *Canada Press*, Oct. 19, 2013

Phillip R. Shaver & Mario Mikulencer, "Dialogue on Adult Attachment: Diversity and Integration," *Attachment and Human Development*, 2002, 4: 133-161

Saltman, Bethany, "Can Attachment Theory Explain All our Relationships," *nymag.com/thecut*

Schore, Judith, & Schore Allan, N., "Modern Attachment Theory: The Central Role of Affect Regulation in Development and Treatment," *Clinical Social Work Journal*, (2008) 36:9-20

Sroufe, Alan, "Attachment and Development: A prospective, longitudinal study from birth to adulthood," *Attachment and Human Development*, December 2005, 7 (4), 349-367

Sroufe, Alan & Siegel, Daniel, "The Verdict is in: The case for attachment Theory," *drdansiegel.com/uploads/1271*

Koren-Karie & Oppenheim, David (Ed.), "Parental Insightfulness: Its role in fostering children's healthy development," in *Attachment and Human Development*, Vol. 20, No.3, June 2018

Zeindler, Christine, "Prenatal Maternal Stress," *Douglas Mental Health University Institute*, Jan. 2013, (online article)

ACKNOWLEDGEMENTS

I am grateful to all the people I have trained and supervised for encouraging me to write this book and to my clients who confirmed my belief in the usefulness of Attachment Theory as I applied it in their therapy.

I want to acknowledge Dr. Daniel Hughes who started me on the journey of exploring the Theory of Attachment and how to apply it to children and families struggling with Attachment issues. I also want to thank the group of therapists in Cobourg, Ontario for creating an environment where we could share our struggles with our cases and learn how to use Attachment Focused Therapy more effectively.

I am grateful to my friend, Heather Chisvin for all her support and guidance during the writing process. Having written and published her own book, Heather understood my frustrations and fears and encouraged me throughout the challenges of writing and publishing a book.

I also want to thank my friend and colleague Harriet Tarshis who took the time to read and edit my book. Her attention to detail and awareness of proper grammar was a gift in the initial editing of the book.

I am grateful to all the researchers and clinicians who provided an abundance of knowledge and experience from which I drew in the writing of this book. I want to particularly thank Dr. Mary Main whose writings attracted me years ago to the Theory of Attachment as it applied to Adults. I am also thankful to Dr. Dan Siegel for his workshops, writings and DVD's which offered so much information on Attachment and the Brain. Dr. Siegel's use of the Adult Attachment Interview as a valuable clinical tool was most helpful and encouraging of my own utilization of it.

I want to thank Dr. David Pederson and his team for the training on the Adult Attachment Interview. His intense workshop was enlightening, humbling and confirming of the value of understanding clients from an Adult Attachment perspective.

I want to thank Guernica Editions and Michael Mirolla for bringing this book to life and all the support during the publication process.

I am forever grateful to my husband, Uri Igra for his understanding of my need to focus on my writing and for his commitment to our relationship with its ruptures and repairs. He has taught me much about love, nurturing and commitment. My daughter, Devra Igra has been my gift in understanding the true meaning of Attachment and unconditional love. My step-son, Noam, has also helped me understand how one can love and be close without a biological connection.

My husband and daughter are both accomplished therapists.

ABOUT THE AUTHOR

Annette Kussin received her first Social Work degree from the University of Manitoba. Having been raised in a Socialist family her initial interest in Social Work was to empower underprivileged people and to work with children and families from disadvantaged neighbourhoods. After working in Neighbourhood Service Centers for some years she changed her focus and worked in a psychiatric centre and a residential treatment centre. She eventually received her Masters in Social Work and specialized for many years in Marriage and Family Therapy.

Annette has worked most of her career in Children's Mental Health as a front-line worker, a supervisor, Head of a Family Therapy Program and a Clinical Director, mainly in Toronto, Ontario. She was the Clinical Director of Oologen Community Services, a CMHC for Adolescents and the Creche Child and Family Centre (now the Child Development Institute), a CMHC for preschool children. As a Clinical Director she offered new directions to the agencies she directed and supervised many managers and staff.

Annette eventually started a private practice in partnership with two other Social Workers. Her partners and she created a successful practice offering training and therapy. Annette began to focus more of her work and understanding on Trauma, Attachment and the Brain. She began developing workshops in this area.

After leaving the partnership, she and her husband created a private therapy centre called The Leaside Therapy Centre. Annette was able to actualize her vision of creating a community of multi-discipline therapists, who could support and refer to one another. The Centre was successful in offering excellent services in a variety of disciplines. Annette had an active private practice at the Centre, providing therapy, consultation and training. After almost a decade Annette and her husband sold the Centre to focus on their therapeutic practices. Annette has continued her private practice to date, focusing on Attachment Focused Therapy, Training and Consultation.

Throughout her career Annette has always challenged herself to grow professionally, learning and practicing new and exciting models of therapy. She has specialized and offered training in Family and Marital Therapy, Trauma related to Sexual Abuse, Custody and Access Assess- ments and Attachment and Brain Development. Her interest in Attach- ment grew initially from her work with preschool children. After studying and working with Dr. Dan Hughes and a group of therapists interested in Attachment Focused Therapy, Annette began to focus her practice on working with adopted children and their families. During this time Annette took many workshops and read many books pub- lished on Attachment, developing her expertise in this area. She met regularly with Dr. Hughes and her colleagues focusing on Attachment issues. This group of therapists developed a consultation group in Attachment Focused Therapy.

Her interest in Adult Attachment grew out of her work with the parents of the adopted children and her work with adults in individual and marital therapy. As Annette became more interested in Adult Attach- ment, she became aware of how little was written in the area of Adult

Attachment for professionals and the public. She became more interested in the research of Mary Main and the development of Dr. Main's questionnaire to determine the Categories of Adult Attachment. Other researchers and clinicians in Attachment work, similar to Annette, are interested in applying this questionnaire for clinicians. Over the years of Annette's interest, more has been written about Adult Attachment as it applies to clinical work and even some books for the general public.

Because of Annette's belief in the usefulness and importance of Adult Attachment as a way of understanding oneself and one's relationships she has developed workshops to encourage other professionals to incorporate an understanding of Adult Attachment in their clinical work. She has offered workshops for many years to many organizations throughout Ontario, Canada, has developed an advanced course in Adult Attachment and offers consultation and supervision to individual therapists and organizations.

Annette has written this book on Adult Attachment for the general public because of her belief that this perspective on understanding oneself and one's relationship is so valuable. There are also so few therapists who offer Attachment Focused Therapy, although the numbers are growing, that people may need to find a way to help themselves from an Attachment perspective.

Annette has many other interests and passions. She has been a hobby potter for over 30 years, loves films, opera and travel. She is an avid jogger and practices Pilates. She travels regularly to Israel to visit her children, grandchildren and friends.

Annette values family and friends and devotes much time to these relationships. She continues to work on her own Attachment issues, knowing this is a lifelong journey.

As Annette moves toward the later stages of her career, she wants to ensure that professionals and the general public have this exciting and powerful perspective on understanding human beings and how they find closeness in relationships.